Property of the U.S. Army

A Vietnam Veteran's Story of Survival and Recovery

Edward B. Adams
As told to Kilee Brookbank

LIBRARY OF CONGRESS CATALOGING-IN-PUBLICATION DATA
Names: Adams, Edward B., 1950- author. | Brookbank, Kilee, 1998- interviewer.
Title: Property of the U.S. Army : a Vietnam veteran's story of survival and recovery / Edward B. Adams, as told to Kilee Brookbank.
Other titles: Vietnam veteran's story of survival and recovery
Description: Georgetown, Ohio : KiCam Projects, [2020] | Summary: ""PROPERTY OF THE U.S. ARMY" They had stamped it on his T-shirt, his footlocker, and the plastic stock of his M-16. Decades later, he'd find they'd stamped it on his soul. Ed was just twenty years old when a Vietcong landmine ripped off both his legs below the knee. After only four months and four days in combat, Ed found himself in a hospital bed fighting for his life - a life he would barely recognize when he returned to his small-town Ohio home. After five decades of struggling through alcoholism, drugs, failed marriages, and physical abuse, Ed shares his story for the first time, processing the lifelong impact of combat ... of coming home to a nation that didn't want him ... of physical and mental wounds that never fully healed. As Ed reveals his truths to readers, he discovers something for himself: that war is hell but that life and liberty are always worth fighting for"-- Provided by publisher.
Identifiers: LCCN 2020034397 (print) | LCCN 2020034398 (ebook) | ISBN 9781734564204 (paperback) | ISBN 9781734564211 (epub)
Subjects: LCSH: Adams, Edward B., 1950- | Vietnam War, 1961-1975--Veterans.
| Veterans--Ohio--Biography. | Amputees--Ohio--Biography.
Classification: LCC DS559.73.U6 A43 2020 (print) | LCC DS559.73.U6 (ebook) | DDC 959.704/34092 [B]--dc23
LC record available at https://lccn.loc.gov/2020034397
LC ebook record available at https://lccn.loc.gov/2020034398

Cover and book design by Mark Sullivan
ISBN 978-1-7345642-0-4 (paperback)
ISBN 978-1-7345642-1-1 (ebook)

Printed in the United States of America
Published by KiCam Projects
Georgetown, Ohio

www.KiCamProjects.com

Dedication

....

This book is dedicated to all who have been wounded in war, especially those who were by my side on that fateful day in Vietnam fifty years ago.

Table of Contents

Preface

General William Tecumseh Sherman, who served under General Ulysses S. Grant — both from Ohio, as I am — during the Civil War, said, "War is hell." And he was right. But what about a "conflict"? The United States never declared war on north Vietnam. But let me tell you: I was there. It was war. And it was hell.

I can't speak for all of the 2.7 million American soldiers who served in Vietnam during the "conflict," but I can't imagine them describing it any other way. I am a double amputee and a proud United States Army veteran, and I am not alone. Seventy-five thousand American soldiers were severely disabled in Vietnam. Amputations or crippling wounds were 300 percent higher in Vietnam than in World War II.

A total of 304,000 American soldiers were wounded in Vietnam, and I am one of them. That's a staggering number of wounded. And we were the lucky ones. Why would I say that? Because 58,220 were killed in action, and many soldiers still remain listed as missing in action. Those young men gave their lives for their country — for all of us. A lot of them were drafted, as I was, and they served and ultimately gave all. Just as it is an honor to be an American citizen, it is an honor to serve this great nation — then, now, and forever.

Time is something we all have. Certainly, some get less time than others, but we are all given a precious gift. How you choose to spend your time on this earth is up to you. In my life, I had a brief moment in time that was decided for me, when I was drafted into the Army. But after my service, I still had plenty of choices to make. Upon reading this book, you might agree that I wasn't a very good decision-maker at times — maybe for quite a long time. I've certainly lived a life full of highs and lows. But I'm lucky to have lived it, and I'm grateful for every moment of it.

Introduction

Man, what a day. Warm, sunny — a typical southern Ohio summer day. I was less than a year out of high school and working at a hardware store in my hometown of Lebanon. You know, for a nineteen-year-old, that was a cool job. I really liked it. I got to see a lot of people I knew when they came into the store, and I got to meet quite a few new folks, as well. It was a small-town hardware store that helped small-town people, like me.

After work, I checked the mailbox at home and saw a letter addressed to me. Written on the outer envelope were the words: "The United States Army." I knew I needed to open it immediately. I went inside to do so with my mother and father around me.

Right away, I saw some scary words in big, bold type.

"Greetings! You have been inducted into the United States Army."

Oh, shit!

My mother started crying while my father tried to console her.

I was in shock. I wasn't sure how a 110-pound-soaking-wet, five-feet-six-inches-tall teen-aged me was going to handle war. All I could think about was how I would survive.

Of course, just like every other red-blooded, proud American — especially young men of draft age, like myself — I'd kept up with what was going on in the Vietnam conflict. I thought I had a pretty good idea of what awaited me over there.

The letter stated the date, time, and location I needed to report for basic training: May 1970. I had about a month of freedom left.

When you get a letter like that, you don't know if you will be back home to see your friends and family again, so I wanted to make the best of the situation. So, after it all sort of sunk in, the first thing that came to mind was beer. And lots of it.

That night, I went out with my friends Deon and Dewayne. The legal drinking age in Ohio in 1970 was eighteen, so we partied and got drunk together. Dewayne was also drafted around the same time. We both needed to get away from life for a little bit. It was good to have someone to talk to who was going through the same thing I was. We went to a bar in our hometown and carried on for hours that night, talking about life, girls, friends, and whatever else kept us in the moment and out of the reality of what we were about to experience.

There is no good way to prepare yourself for war. So, I did what felt good to me at that moment — I partied. I'm sure a lot of men my age reacted the same way. Was it the right thing or best thing to do? I don't know. *Is* there a right way to respond when you're told you've been chosen to travel thousands of miles away from home to possibly have to kill strangers in a jungle?

All I knew for sure was that partying allowed me to spend time with people I might not see again. And it got my mind off war for a while.

I'd always felt a sense of duty when it came to the war. I knew it was right to do for my country, but I had mixed feelings. I didn't feel prepared. I didn't want to leave my family and friends. When I told them I was drafted, many felt the same way I did. But there were some who encouraged me to get out of going to war. I was in a relationship with a girl named Jane. She was a few years younger and still in high school, so I was teased a lot for "robbing the cradle." Her parents didn't like that she was dating an older man, so we didn't see each other much. When we did see each other, we had to sneak around. Jane didn't want me to go to war; she thought I should flee to Canada.

That was the only "easy" way out of fighting in Vietnam, because Canada would not allow you to be extradited back to the United States. I wasn't interested in going to Canada, though, because I knew I would be doing a disservice to my duty. Back then, our history classes taught patriotism. As a U.S. citizen, I knew I needed to honor and serve.

• • •

When I turned eighteen, I had to do a physical examination so the government could make sure I was able to fight. They did this with every man who had to enter the draft when they came of age. There were about fifty guys in the room getting their physical the same time I did. The doctors checked all kinds of things: our eyes, our blood pressure, our reflexes, and so on.

And of course, we had to bend over. Needless to say, none of us guys reacted very well when we were told to bend over and touch our ankles. We looked around at each other with confusion and more than a little embarrassment. *What the hell? Do they really need us to do this?*

The first guy in line had his own approach. He walked right up to the doctor and immediately bent over to show "Kiss my ass" written on his backside. We all got a laugh out of that. Not knowing the entire process, or exactly what they were trying to figure out through this examination, a lot of us were thinking the same thing! But this guy said it for us, right on his ass — and quite proudly, I would add.

I was hoping I wouldn't reach the required weight to be in the Army. I was a small man, and the day of my first physical, I hadn't yet received my draft letter. I had to do the same exam after I got my letter to make sure I was still fit to go to war. In that second physical, it felt more real. If I failed that one, I wouldn't have to go.

The minimum weight for my height was 109 pounds. My dad had been 105 pounds, five-feet-five, and had been exempt from fighting because of his size. No such luck for me.

I made it into the Army by one pound. Even though I was very small, the Army wanted me to fight.

So now, the Army owned me — same as they owned the "Kiss my ass" guy. Little did I know, in just a few short months, I would be returning from Vietnam with injuries that would define how I would live my life forever.

Chapter One

The Day My Life Changed

We weren't supposed to be there. But our captain wanted us to patrol the area one more time. Our job was to find the North Vietnamese army and report where they were so we could send bombs and helicopters to take them out.

The day before we went on that last patrol, I'd heard that a lot of people were being medevacked out of the battlefield. We were pretty far away from the group that was getting hit hard. Our captain said we needed to find that group and help them, since they were surrounded by the North Vietnamese. It was hot and we had to walk two or three klicks (kilometers) to get there. We were tired and our feet were worn out because we had to move so quickly. When we finally reached them, they no longer needed us. Typical.

The captain was a gung-ho kind of guy. He didn't want the North Vietnamese to win. He decided we should go out on patrol again the next day to that same location.

After hearing about people in our company getting hit hard, all I could think about was when it would be my turn to be injured in battle. It's hard not to think about that stuff when that's all you see and hear about. It's hard to have positive thoughts of any kind in that situation. It's the harsh reality of war: little to no sleep, tediously taking each step, ready for the next shot to be fired, and hoping like hell it won't hit you or anyone around you. Nobody wants to be injured, but the fact of war is that those things happen.

It was a clear, sunny day — much like the day I received my draft letter. The sun was about to set when we began patrolling. We were walking through the jungle when someone came over the radio telling our captain to leave the area. There were North Vietnamese all around us. Our captain was told it was too unsafe to be there, but he didn't want to leave. In other words, there was a high probability a lot of heavy shit was about to happen.

We continued walking through the jungle until our point man looked back at us.

"Bring the dog. We spotted something."

Our scout dogs were highly trained to find and attack the enemy. I was near the dog and its handler when they walked past the point man. Then …

Everything stopped and my ears were ringing. I must have been right on top of the explosion. I think I was blown six or seven feet in the air. Most of the fragments of the mine scattered around me, shooting shrapnel in every direction. My ears had been ringing for a couple minutes. I heard gunshots and people yelling, and smoke was everywhere. When I landed back on the ground, I didn't feel anything. I passed out for a little bit.

I saw a man. He was dressed in white and had a long beard. He said to me, "Don't worry, Ed, you'll make it." Was it God telling me I would survive? To this day I can't say for sure, but I believe it was.

I woke up after that. I looked down at one of my legs and all I could see was bones. I didn't look at the other leg; I guess I didn't want to know what it looked like after seeing the first one. Besides, it was chaos all over. I saw people in my platoon lying on the ground injured, and I couldn't help them.

I was in shock — and in so much pain. I registered almost nothing besides the smell. I vividly remember the stink of battle. It was a suffocating mix of acrid smoke and gunpowder — like fireworks — combined with that steamy, heavy, rotting odor of the jungle. It made me feel like I couldn't breathe. Trust me, it's a stench you never want to experience. All I could think about in that moment was getting to the hospital.

To say the situation was bad is an understatement. We still had to defend our position, but we felt helpless.

In the middle of everything, I overheard the captain, who was a few feet away from me, talking to his radio. The radio man had been killed, so our captain took it into his own hands to notify our company that we had been in battle and needed a medevac immediately.

"You've got to get down here!" he yelled.

He gave our coordinates and a brief run-down of what had just happened. It was a dire situation.

The medevac told him they couldn't come to our area because there was too much incoming gunfire. We were still under attack. But the captain wouldn't let up. Finally, he persuaded them to come get us. I don't recall his exact words, but they included some expletives and enough urgency to convince them it was a risk they had to take. If they didn't come, it was certain death for all of us.

After our captain had sorted everything out and put the radio down, I looked over at him and noticed something: His legs were gone, too. I was amazed he could continue to lead and try to protect our company while he was lying on the ground near death, like I was.

We waited about twenty-five minutes for the medevac to arrive. That whole time, I lay there thinking about what I needed to do to survive. I guess as animals, we have an instinct that kicks in when we're in danger.

The helicopter couldn't land on the ground because of the vegetation that surrounded the area, so they motioned for us to climb up. There was gunfire from almost every direction. The guys still able to defend our position were fighting furiously. This was the only way out while we were still alive.

One of the guys in my platoon who wasn't injured helped me get up into the helicopter. He helped me grab onto the skids, and one of the medics inside took my arm and pulled me in. He asked me, "How are you doing, Ed?" — he'd obviously read my dog tags to find my name and blood type — and quickly got to work trying to save my life. He laid me down and put tourniquets on my legs to stop the blood flow. That's when I thought to myself, *Oh, no, it's bad now.*

He kept telling me, "Don't go to sleep. Stay awake." I never did go to sleep.

The helicopter ride out felt like forever. I was in excruciating pain. I couldn't think straight. The guys in the helicopter were working on me. I don't know what they were doing to me, but to keep my mind off it all, I watched out the window. We were low to the ground so I could see all the rice paddies we were flying over. It was the only thing I could look at to try to keep my mind off what was happening around me.

There were guys shooting at the ground from the helicopter, trying to defend our troops while we were flying through the air. They eventually stopped after we got far enough away from the battlefield.

The hospital was about thirty minutes away from where the helicopter picked us up. There were six of us who'd made it onboard. They sent another medevac for the rest of the guys who were still on the ground.

They took me into the rear area of the hospital where they laid me on the gurney and started working on me. I was immediately poked with a needle, and that was the last thing I remember from that day. I was put in an induced coma to minimize my pain.

Three days later, I woke up.

Geez, I'm in a hospital. I'm still alive, I thought.

I looked down and saw I didn't have legs. I thought to myself, *I don't have feet, but I'm still alive.*

When they'd poked me with that needle, I wasn't sure I'd ever wake up again. So, lying there, I was grateful. I was still in a lot of pain and I knew my life would never be the same again, but I was thankful I wasn't dead.

Of the eighteen people in my squad on that mission that day, nine were killed or injured. I think that's what made me grateful. Knowing I could have been killed put things into perspective early on.

Chapter Two

Growing Up Easy

I grew up dreaming of being a policeman or a firefighter. It was that way from the time I was a little boy to the time I was in high school. I don't know why it appealed to me so much. Maybe because when we were younger, we would pretend to be policemen and firefighters on the playground. As I got older, those dreams faded away.

My childhood was pretty easy. Mom and Dad never let us go without. Dad worked all day and came home to a meal made by Mom, and my brother and I went to school. That was the typical middle-class family back then.

I was close with Mom because she was always around. Dad was always working and never had time for play. He worked for Frigidaire Corp., a large appliance factory, which was a good factory job to have in our area. He worked a lot of overtime; if they offered it, he worked it. In factory work, you never know when they'll decide to change things. Different shifts, benefit cuts, or whatever the case may be, he knew working overtime was something he needed to do. Of course, back then, as a kid, I didn't always understand why he worked so much, but as I got older, I appreciated the sacrifices he made for our family.

One thing my dad and I spent time doing together was collecting coins. That was our thing. Dad was always fascinated with coins, and he introduced me to collecting them because they were still made of silver back then.

Dad would come home from work and pick all the coins out of his pockets for us to check. He would lay them out on the dining room table, and we would pick through, one by one, to see if they were of any value. It was always exciting when he would come home and empty his pockets. I'm still interested in collecting coins, and to this day I have many of the coins he and I collected together.

I have an older brother named Lee. We don't have a lot in common — even as a kid, my brother and I weren't very close. We always had different interests and friends, even though we were only two and a half years apart. Lee was never into sports and staying fit like I was. He stuck with his friends, and I stuck with mine. And that was the way it was until he moved out.

When we were young, Mom and Dad had only one car. Dad drove the car to work, so after Lee and I came home from school, we were pretty much stranded there. Mom hardly ever left home, and when she did, it was when we were all four together. Every other weekend, we would go to Kentucky to see my parents' relatives. They were both from central Kentucky and their families lived near each other. We had a lot of fun when we would go there, because our cousins were around our age.

Back in those days, we didn't have phones or Internet to pass our time. We spent our time meeting up with friends and playing games outside. We would invite our friends over after school and find something to do. We would play anything that could be played outdoors: hide and seek, Wiffle ball, or just exploring the woods. If it could be done outside, we did it. It was always fun to adventure outside. It seemed like a game to us to see what we could find. Whoever found the coolest object would win bragging rights for a little bit. When we weren't outside, we would play a lot of board games, like Monopoly, Clue, Scrabble, and Battlefield.

We had so much fun back then, and I sometimes wonder if kids these days understand what they're missing out on.

When I was in middle school, I met my best friend, Deon. We were in a lot of the same classes, and we just hit it off. After getting to know each other a little bit, we realized we only lived about a mile apart. We lived on connecting country roads, which made it easy to ride our bikes to each other's houses. Deon was a big guy. He kept me from getting beat up. I was never bullied, but when Deon would get us into trouble with other kids our age, I felt safe because I knew no one would mess with him. We stayed friends all throughout middle school and high school, and we are still friends today. Deon is one of those guys you can always depend on. To this day, outside of my family, Deon is my first phone call, whether it's just to say hello or whatever it may be. I can count on him, and he knows he can always count on me.

• • •

When I was in middle school, Mom started working again. Before she went to work, she was the one who took care of us and the house. Lee and I had to start doing chores. We cleaned the house, did the dishes, and washed our clothes. I guess Mom thought it was time we learn about responsibility since I was twelve and Lee was fourteen. We ate a lot of TV dinners then because neither my brother nor I could cook. For a while, it was cool to eat a TV dinner. They were a big thing when they first came out. The best thing about them: They were easy to fix. Of course, they're even easier to fix today — just pop them in the microwave for a few minutes and they're finished. When Lee and I made them, you had to cook them in the oven for about forty-five minutes!

To earn some extra money, I helped out the neighbors. I cleaned chicken coops, babysat, and housesat. The neighbors were farmers and they were always nice to my family. They helped us out when we needed it.

When I was a kid, it was common to have a cistern, or well, for water. We'd have to pump water to the house for cooking, baths, and drinking water. It wasn't particularly hard work, but it was something that had to be done on a regular basis. I wasn't big enough to pump the well behind our house, so Lee or Dad would be the one to do that job. By the time I was old enough and big enough to pump the well, we didn't use it that often. That's one job Lee always got to do and got compensated for in some way. I guess that's what I got for being smaller and younger.

The Vietnam War was going on when I was in eighth grade. My classmates and I would discuss what our futures held, and even though we were still young, we were paranoid about the war. We all hoped it would end before we graduated so we didn't have to be involved. The thought that ran through my mind was, *Am I going to get drafted or not? What will I do if I get to that point?*

We talked about it a lot, but there was nothing any of us could say that would make us feel better. Deon's older brother had been drafted and served in Vietnam. I never really knew him that well before he went to the war, but Deon said he was never the same when he came home. Deon's brother was fortunate to make it home without injury, but that doesn't mean he wasn't scarred. He bore the internal, emotional scars for the rest of his life. He fell into drug addiction and remained in that state of mind for several years. He died of AIDS when he was in his late fifties. Deon never talked much about his brother, other than to say he just wasn't the same after Vietnam. Maybe the reason Deon didn't talk much about him was the fact that the brother he knew had been gone for a long time. As for Deon, he was never drafted due to the fact he didn't pass the physical. He has high blood pressure. Even as a teenager, his blood pressure was bad enough that it kept him from being eligible for the draft.

• • •

When I got to Springboro High School, I started working out because I knew my size could impact sports I might play.

At five feet six and a hundred pounds, to say I was small is an understatement! For some reason, I decided to join the wrestling team. I'm not sure where I came up with that idea, but I think it had something to do with my newfound love of weightlifting. I didn't like that so many people were bigger than me. I felt like I couldn't protect myself. Once I started weightlifting, it came naturally to me. It was like I was meant to do it.

I could lift ninety pounds over my head with one hand, then lift the other ninety-pound weight in the other hand. One day, Deon decided he wanted to have a weightlifting competition. I told him he was going to lose, but since he was bigger, he thought he had won before we even started. We kept adding more weight to the bench-press bar to see who could lift more. I eventually won, and he got so mad. He couldn't believe I could lift that much weight! I think all my weight training helped me prepare myself for wrestling. Not only did it help me win matches, but it was fun.

Back then, wrestling was an intramural event. It wasn't like it is today. We didn't compete with other schools or have tournaments. We just competed with people within our school. I was the best at wrestling, undefeated in the feather-weight class.

The track coach tried to get me to run, but I was never interested, partly because I knew my parents couldn't take me to the meets and practices. Instead of running around the track, I chose to run around my house. Some days I would run a hundred laps. I liked to run outside, and it kept me fit, which helped with wrestling.

Lots of people admired Arnold Schwarzenegger at the time. He was this new bodybuilder winning competitions all over the world when most of the world had never seen something like that before. He was young and seemed cool, which made him easy to look up to. Arnold was my idol. I wanted to be strong and work out like he did. That is what inspired me to lift, any time I had spare time on my hands.

In gym class, I was the one to beat. When we played dodgeball, I was always one of the last ones standing because I was quick and could get out of the way. I even impressed my teacher once when he criticized my push-ups.

He said, "Ed, I didn't see you do your push-ups correctly. Give me twenty more."

"Fine! I can do more than twenty."

I got on the ground and did eighty push-ups. My gym teacher didn't bother me again.

Looking back on my athleticism in high school, I think I was preparing myself for what was to come without knowing that these things I trained myself to do would come in handy one day.

• • •

I had grown up with some responsibility, but in high school, I just wanted to party with my friends and flirt with all the girls. My friends and I would go to drive-in restaurants to eat, then go hot-rod on the backroads. When we weren't eating or hot-rodding, we would go to a friend's house to drink and party. Sometimes we made room for doing things that weren't dangerous, like going to a drive-in movie. Things are a lot different now. Back then, it was easy for us to hot-rod on back roads because there weren't many cars around. It wasn't hard to get alcohol because the drinking age was eighteen, and even that wasn't as heavily enforced as it is now. Life is just a lot busier and more fast-paced today.

When I was seventeen, I decided it was time to stop riding my bike around town. I got my license and it was perfect timing. Lee had just gotten himself a new car and didn't need his anymore. He gave it back to Mom and Dad and they decided it could be mine. It was a dark blue 1962 Chevrolet Corvair. It wasn't the best car in the world, but it got me where I needed to go. I was thankful my parents and my brother were willing to help me out. If Lee hadn't bought a new car, I would probably have still been riding my bike everywhere. My parents had bought the car a few years earlier for about a thousand dollars. That was quite a buy back then, probably equivalent to spending $10,000 nowadays.

Good ol' Deon's first car was an AMC Rambler. We were both proud to finally have our driver's licenses and our own cars to drive. We enjoyed our first taste of freedom and the sense of responsibility that goes along with that privilege.

All throughout high school, my grades were all right. I usually made C's. School wasn't too hard for me; I just didn't apply myself. I knew I wasn't going to college, so I didn't really care what my grades were. College wasn't something everyone did or was expected to do. It was only for the people who had money. Mom and Dad didn't have the money to send Lee and me to college, so we never even thought about it. College wasn't like it is now. No one borrowed money to go to school back then. If you or your parents didn't have the money to send you, you weren't going.

. . .

Like I said, I was into girls much of my high school career. My class was about 130 students, so there were plenty of girls to choose from. In my junior year, I met Jane. She was pretty, nice, and was fine with hanging out with my friends. She was only in eighth grade and we went to different schools, so we didn't see each other much. But when we did, we got along well. We talked about our future and even discussed being together after she graduated high school.

Jane and I met through Deon's girlfriend at a school dance and kept in touch afterward. We had similar interests and similar friends, so the relationship seemed easy. Because we lived about an hour away from each other, Deon's girlfriend was Jane's cover when we found time to go out together. Jane would tell her parents she was going to meet her friend, but really she would meet me somewhere.

While Jane and I were dating, I went out with other girls occasionally. It wasn't that I didn't like Jane, I just didn't see her very often — and I didn't know what she was doing when we weren't together. The only form of communication we ever really had, besides in-person conversations, was letters. We didn't use phones much back then.

I only seriously dated one other girl while I was with Jane. Her name was Caroline and she was only in town during the summers. She lived in Indiana, but her family visited her aunt's house near mine every summer. After knowing each other for a couple of years, Caroline and I got pretty serious the summer before my senior year, 1968. Caroline and I spent a lot of time together — unlike Jane and me. I even got her a promise ring. When she left to go back to Indiana, we agreed we would continue dating long-distance.

At the time, I was glad I had bought her the ring; it made me feel somewhat special that she could wear it while being hundreds of miles away, and I hoped it would remind her of me each time she looked at it. Back then, giving or receiving a promise ring was a big deal. When you had a "steady" girlfriend, you normally gave her your class ring to wear. As things progressed in the relationship, the next step was the coveted promise ring, or "pre-engagement" ring as we called it. After that, it got really serious, the real deal ... an actual engagement ring. The fact that I skipped step one and went straight to step two made me feel like quite the ladies' man! The ring itself was a serious purchase — $100. Fifty-something years ago, that wasn't chump change. I felt I had "stepped up" to buy such an expensive piece of jewelry. I can't recall exactly, but I either ordered it from the Sears catalog or bought it at Montgomery Ward. It had to be one of those two options, simply because they were the only options. The ring was gold with a small diamond — and "small" is probably being generous. Now that I'm a little older, I would probably need a magnifying glass to see it! Nonetheless, I bought it, Caroline accepted it, and we were both happy about it.

But one weekend that following fall, I made the drive to Indiana to see Caroline. We had a good time together, but I couldn't see our relationship lasting. We lived so far from each other that it was unrealistic. I went back home, and about a week after I visited Caroline, I received a letter from her. She said we lived too far apart and that she had started seeing someone else. She sent the promise ring back with the letter, and that was the last I heard from her for years. I don't remember now what I did with that ring.

Jane and I continued dating throughout the rest of my time in high school. We went to prom together and kept in contact when we could. It was a comfortable relationship and we did love each other, despite my actions with other girls.

• • •

Deon and I were friends through everything. We were together almost all the time, and we managed to do some pretty dumb stuff.

One day, we were in Deon's family's barn, and Deon convinced me we should shoot each other with a BB gun. It was like the scene out of *A Christmas Story*, where Ralphie almost shoots his eye out. Of course, Deon persuaded me to be shot first. As soon as Deon pulled the trigger, I knew I never should have agreed to that. I felt the BB on my hand and immediately yelled, "Ow! Deon!" He just looked at me with a smirk and started laughing.

"I'm done with this," I said. "You're going to plum knock an eye out!"

All Deon could do was crack up. I tried to shoot him back, but I missed. I wish I would have hit him, because it seemed like he found a lot of joy in my pain. He might even have intentionally introduced this game because he knew I would miss him.

Deon was a little bit of a bully. I couldn't say anything to him about it because I didn't want to hurt our friendship. He picked on other people — and even me sometimes. His bullying always got us into trouble, especially after we both were able to drive. On a few occasions, I'd be driving and Deon would hang out of the passenger window, flipping off and cussing at the people behind us. One night when Deon was up to his antics, the car he was bothering kept following us, and I was afraid something might happen. Fortunately, I saw a coach from school driving up ahead of us, and I followed him to his driveway in the hopes he would protect us. When we got there, I got out of the car and tried to make peace with the guys driving behind us, while also trying to calm Deon down. Somehow, I was the one who got punched in the face! My reward for playing peacemaker? A black eye.

The coach took care of me and let us come into his house after telling the other guys to get out of his driveway. I was thankful he was willing to help us after what Deon had done.

Deon and I found ourselves in self-induced panic mode more than once. It was usually due to being ornery. Next thing you'd know, there we were again, trying to get ourselves out of a bad situation and, ultimately, out of whatever trouble might follow. For my size, I could hold my own. I also knew Deon would always have my back when I needed it. We got into mischief a lot, but nothing too serious. We were just young men living life. We're still like that today; the only difference is, we're no longer young.

• • •

I was fifteen or sixteen when I found myself in quite a predicament due to no fault of my own. I used to work for a guy who had a small farm. I did odd jobs such as cleaning barns, mending fences, clearing weeds — basically whatever was needed on a particular day. The farmer I was working for was in his early thirties. He was always polite, paid me when I needed, made sure I had water to drink on hot days, etc. One day, he invited me in the house. He told me he was going to shower and would be right out. In the meantime, I just waited for my next job to do. Well, the next task at hand, I was *not* prepared for nor willing to do! The farmer returned from showering and made sexual advances toward me. He was much bigger than me, so I knew if I allowed him to get too close to me, I would not be able to escape. I bolted out the door as fast as I could, and where did I go? Straight to Deon's house. I told him what had happened, and as the good friend he was, he laughed. I never saw the farmer again. I also never mentioned it to anyone else, and to the best of my knowledge, neither has Deon. Until now, the only people who knew this happened were Deon, myself, and of course the farmer.

Was keeping it a secret the right thing to do? Back then, I didn't know what the right thing to do was. So, out of fear of embarrassment, I chose to keep it to myself. Of course, knowing what I do now, and being an adult, I would encourage someone to speak out against that type of situation. Especially as a father, I would want my kids to let the proper people or authorities know. The fact that I was able to leave without incident didn't mean it couldn't have happened to someone else. I can't imagine how my parents would have felt or what they would have done if they'd known what happened.

• • •

When graduation day came, I was happy to be done with high school. At the same time, we all knew what could come in the mail within the next few days, weeks, or months. I tried to keep all of that out of my mind. Instead of worrying about what could be, I focused on what was happening in my life right then and there.

I went to graduation parties for two weeks straight. There was a party every night. At the parties, we sat around a bonfire, talked, and drank beer. Beer was the biggest thing, since we could buy our own. Kids our age were only allowed to buy beer that had a lower alcohol percentage, called 3.2 beer. It tasted gross and didn't get us as drunk, so we'd ask older people to buy us the good stuff.

It was a bittersweet time. I was a little sad that we were graduating, because I didn't want to leave my friends behind. We had been together for so long and knew so much about one another. Now, we didn't know what the future held or what the next chapters of our lives would look like.

• • •

I got the job at Ted's Hardware and Rental because I was too small for the factory jobs that paid more money. The hardware store was fun. I got to interact with people every day, and it kept me entertained while giving me a paycheck. I was still living at home because I didn't have enough money to move out. My parents liked the company. Dad still wasn't home much, and Mom liked having me around for dinner.

My friends who worked in factories made between $3.60 to $4 per hour. The major employers in our area were General Motors, Ford, and Frigidaire, where Dad worked for more than thirty years. The factory positions were mostly assembly line jobs, which I was told had size requirements. I figured I wouldn't be qualified to work there, so I never applied.

At the hardware store, I made a respectable $1.80 per hour. That's quite a difference, but I really did like it. I've often asked myself what I would have done if I hadn't been drafted, and I really think I would have stayed at the hardware store. To work there, you needed basic knowledge of trades such as plumbing, electrical, carpentry, etc. Eventually I might have found myself working in one of those types of jobs. That appealed to me, because unlike factory jobs, you aren't going to the same place day in, day out. Just like my job at the hardware store, I would have met new people each week and would have had the opportunity to work in different surroundings with each project.

All the while, I was worried about the draft and being called for duty. I didn't want to go to war. No one did. My friends and I talked about it, but Mom and Dad didn't discuss it much. I'm sure they were trying to keep it off their minds, too, but I wish they would have had conversations with me about it. It might have prepared me better or made me feel more at ease. At the time, though, it seemed pointless to talk about it if there were no definite answers until you got the letter.

There were lots of people who were against the war. I didn't want to be one of those people they called "baby killers" because they were forced to go to Vietnam. My life was good. I didn't want it to be ruined by war and all that comes with it.

Once I got the draft letter, I knew my life would change forever. I just held onto the hope that I would make it back home one day.

Chapter Three

Basic Training

There was a lottery for the draft on December 1, 1969. Numbers were assigned based on a person's birthday. The government had 366 small blue capsules that had a note with a day of the year on them. The government hand-drew each capsule from a jar and continued until all days of the year were assigned to a lottery number.

The first date called was September 14, which meant that all men born on that day between 1944 and 1950 were assigned to lottery number one. Based on how many people were drafted, the government would choose a number as the cutoff.

The night they were announcing the numbers, my friends and I went to the gas station in town where we would sometimes hang out. There were about five or six of us. All of us were hoping we would have high numbers. We were scared as we listened around the radio inside the gas station.

I was nervous the whole time we waited. Every time I would hear another date called that wasn't my birthday, I felt a sense of relief, but I knew it wasn't over yet. I listened to 179 dates until I finally heard the one I didn't want to hear. When my birthday — March 1 — was called out, I didn't know exactly what to think. I held onto the little hope I had that I wouldn't have to go because my number was relatively high. At the same time, I was thinking about what I would do if I had to go to war.

Around the mid-200s and up probably would escape the war altogether. My number was 180.

My friends at the gas station all got higher numbers than I had. When they didn't hear their birthdays being called out, they were happy. When my birthday was called, we all paused and looked at each other. Nothing was said. We just sat in silence and listened for the next birthday to be called.

The rest of the night, I was sad. I didn't know what the future held for me. I couldn't help but be envious of my friends. They didn't have to worry about their futures.

• • •

I didn't receive my basic training letter until early April 1970. The whole time in between, I just waited for it to show up in our mailbox. I knew in my heart there was no way I wouldn't be drafted. I had a feeling it didn't matter if I hoped for anything.

I continued working at the hardware store and seeing my friends and Jane. Every day after I got home from work, I checked the mail to see if I had been called for duty. When that day finally came, I couldn't be all that shocked. I had a gut feeling I wasn't going to get out of it as easily as my brother did.

Lee had been dating the same girl since high school. Shortly after they graduated, they got married. Then shortly after that, she got pregnant. To this day, I still don't know if he rushed all those things to get out of war. I have always had a feeling that's what happened. Whether it was on purpose or not, it seemed like Lee was taking the easy way out. A little part of me always felt it was unfair that I had to go and he didn't.

• • •

On April 23, 1970, I was inducted into basic training in Fort Knox, Kentucky. When I arrived at the base, I was scared to death. I thought to myself, *Why do they want me here? I am so much smaller than these guys.* As I looked around, I saw many men who were much bigger than I was. That was the story of my life, but this time I felt terribly out of place, like I just wasn't supposed to be there.

They didn't give us much time to settle in. The first thing they did was cut our hair off. Back then, it was cool for guys to have longer hair. My hair was pretty long, almost down to my shoulders. I didn't really want it cut, but by the time it happened, I had more important things to worry about. There were so many new and different things happening. I had a lot to learn and get used to.

Once all our hair was gone, they gave us our clothes, then put us in our first formation. None of us knew what we were doing. We tried our best to blend in and not draw attention to ourselves. I think the point of this was to introduce us to what we would be doing every single day for the next ten weeks. We didn't stay long in our formation, just long enough for us to see what we should do. When we were done with that, they started giving us shots. I guess because we would be living in such close quarters, and because we would be going overseas, we had to be vaccinated.

The worst part of my first day at basic was that I had kitchen duty. They called it KP, kitchen police. They chose who had KP based on alphabetical order, and of course, my name starts with "A." We had to clean the kitchen spotless — wipe the counters, clean the dishes, mop the floors, and put everything back where it came from. I hadn't even thought about this being part of my duties in the Army.

Later in the day, they made us march around. They once again introduced us to something we would do every day for the next ten weeks. We tried to march in formation for a little bit, but no one knew how to do it right. Eventually we moved on and they assigned us each a weapon. We had guns that we had to practice running around and doing physical training with. We weren't allowed to shoot the guns, and there were no bullets in them. They were just there so we would know how it feels to run with heavy equipment strapped to our bodies. There were only a handful of times when we were allowed to practice shooting the M16.

When I finally was able to lie down after the long first day, my mind raced. I was in an uncomfortable setting I didn't know much about. The only thing that made me feel a little better was knowing one of my best friends was with me.

Dewayne and I had talked about how we would be leaving around the same time. But he and I didn't know we were supposed to report to the same base. I didn't see Dewayne until we arrived in Fort Knox. I was surprised and happy to see him. At least I knew someone there and didn't feel completely alone. When we were assigned our platoon, Dewayne and I got lucky and were assigned to the same one. We ended up bunking together. He slept in the bunk above and I slept in the one below. We weren't together all the time, but when we were together, I felt more comfortable.

Coincidentally, another guy I graduated with, Freddy, ended up in the same basic training in Fort Knox. Freddy and I were never really good friends in high school. We just didn't hang around the same people. Still, I thought it was neat that Freddy, Dewayne, and I were all in the same location. It made me feel more at home.

I didn't know what to expect from basic training. I was being thrown into this setting that I could have never imagined. Thinking that in the next few months I would be at war in an unfamiliar country was hard to swallow. I didn't want to kill people, but they pounded it into our heads at basic that we were to kill the enemy — no questions asked. They pounded it so hard in our heads that it was almost impossible to think about the enemy as humans. They separated our feelings from the situation. Most of us just got used to it and didn't think anything of it after we had been hearing it for so long.

People already had been talking that way at home, too. Young soldiers like me came to understand the North Vietnamese had to be dealt with or they might take over the whole world. We were there to stop communism from spreading. The news said so, plenty of Americans said so, and now our drill instructors said so. They definitely brainwashed us a little; it's hard to say how much I truly believed in my heart and how much I "learned" to believe from the Army. I do know that at least some of what I was taught back then sticks with me to this day, some for better and some for worse.

• • •

Basic was tough. The physical and mental pressure we had to go through was enough to make any man go crazy. Of course, we didn't go crazy because we couldn't. We would be punished if we did anything out of the ordinary. Once I was punished because I woke up late and didn't have time to shave before we met with our company. The drill sergeant made me dry shave in front of the entire company of about a hundred people. They all watched as I sliced my face open in multiple tiny cuts with a razor. That was the kind of petty stuff they made us do if we didn't do everything exactly the way they wanted.

Our routine consisted of waking up at 5 a.m., getting ready — which included shaving every morning — meeting our company for the day, and spending all day training. Each day was different when it came to training. Some days we ran and did physical training, and some days we worked on our marching. Some days we had classes all day about guns, war, and combat. Sometimes our days consisted of a mixture of all of those.

Most of the time, we wouldn't get back to our bunks until after 11 p.m. Once we got back from our long day, we would still have to clean our clothes, shoes, and ourselves before we could go to bed. Everything was to be spotless. We were lucky if we got four hours of sleep a night. Of course, all of that was intentional. We were supposed to be preparing ourselves for war. Most likely, four hours or more of sleep is not realistic in the middle of a war zone. They trained us to be able to function on little to no sleep. Sometimes when we had KP duty or guard duty, we had to do it all night and didn't get the chance to go to sleep at all. It was all about structure and having the right mind-set to handle anything and everything that was thrown at us. At the time, we probably didn't realize that keeping our barracks, clothes, boots, weapons, floors, and every other inch of our surroundings spot-free was a proven way of war preparation, but it was. We were to keep going, pushed to the limit both mentally and physically until it seemed normal, until it didn't feel like you were being pushed — it was just another day.

Our shoes had to be spit-shined and spotless. Even though we were just going to dirty them again the next day, we had to take time every night to clean our shoes. It was hard to get sleep with everything we had to do before bed. Sometimes people would be so exhausted that they collapsed.

I had something similar happen to me. I was walking in the woods when we were out training and I fell to the ground. I don't know what happened to me; I just knew I couldn't go anymore. One of the guys from my squad told the sergeant I was having trouble. "My ankle doesn't feel right," I explained. "It gave out when I was walking."

A guy helped me back to see a doctor. The doctor checked me out and told me I had tendinitis. They let me rest for the remainder of the day. The next day, I didn't feel much better, but I knew I couldn't milk it for too long. I continued training the next day. I pushed through my pain. At some point, I had acquired the mind-set that I should keep going no matter what. The Army wanted each person to believe that they could push through anything. Obviously, being in the midst of war is different from basic training, but I feel I learned what it was like to truly fight through anything when I had my issue with tendinitis.

• • •

We got three meals a day, and they weren't the greatest. We didn't complain a lot about them, but they definitely weren't Mom's home-cooked meals. The food must have been decently good, though, because I somehow gained between five and ten pounds! That was a lot for me, because I was always small and never gained weight. It might have also been all the working out we had to do daily. I think the Army's goal was to have everyone in basic bulk up.

After basic, the first meal I had back home was fried chicken. That tasted like heaven compared to those Army cafeteria meals. Thinking about it now, they probably fed us not-so-great food because they wanted us to get used to eating whatever filled our stomachs. There was no room for picky eaters in the military.

Some days were more intense than others. To learn what it was like in war, we had to practice being in that setting. One of our exercises was a staged battlefield, with live rounds going off six feet above our heads as we were crawling and walking around. There were bombs in the ground, and people were shooting guns all around us. It definitely gave me a good scare!

The idea was to prepare us for being in live fire. Nothing could fully prepare you for actual combat, but that little taste of the experience was enough for me. If I hadn't been nervous about going to Vietnam before that, I sure was afterward.

At one point, I became the squad leader. Being the squad leader meant being in charge of about ten people. There were only four squad leaders total, so I must have done something right to get myself one of those positions. I had to make sure everyone's stuff was clean and ready to go. I don't think I was a tough squad leader. I was pretty easy-going. Ironically, Dewayne ended up being in my squad. This was quite the change for our friendship. Usually Dewayne was the one bossing me around and telling me what we were doing. This time, I was in charge of Dewayne. I don't think he liked it too much.

I kept thinking to myself, *Wow! I'm the smallest guy and somehow I'm the squad leader.* I never thought I would have a role that meant being in charge of people. I always thought of myself as the person who would be bossed around — not the boss. It was cool to order people around. The only thing that made me feel bad was that I had to boss around my friend. We made jokes out of it after it was all said and done. He picked on me and I picked on him. It was our relationship.

• • •

We weren't allowed to call home much. They did let us write letters, but when we did, we were taking time away from sleeping, because it was the only down time we had. I wrote a few letters to Jane and she wrote a few back. The first phone call I made was five weeks into basic training. They didn't want us to call because they didn't want you to get in your own head. My first phone call was to Mom. We talked about how I had been and what had been going on at home. I told her I missed her and Dad and how I couldn't wait until I could come back home. After I got off the phone with her, I called Jane. I told her I was thankful that she was still there for me, and she assured me she wasn't going to leave me hanging.

I was happy to be able to call home. I definitely missed being there and I wished things were different, but I'd accepted the fact that this was my life and this was how it was going to have to be. I was still nervous about my future, but I think basic helped put my mind at ease. Our instructors taught us to feel proud that we were doing something good, fighting communism and fighting for our country. I felt like I was doing an honorable thing, something that would make a difference for America and for the world.

• • •

The first time I was allowed to throw a hand grenade, I was nervous but excited. I had all of this training under my belt and had been in basic for quite some time. I was ready to get to do things with real action. The sergeant had us all lined up. When it was my turn, I went up to throw the hand grenade over the wall, and it just barely made it over. There was a bunker hole right near where I was standing, just in case someone didn't get the grenade over the wall. The sergeant grabbed me and threw me in the hole.

After the grenade blew up, he looked at me and said, "Okay, Adams, you ain't doing that anymore. Get out of here!"

I left and went to work on something else. Everybody laughed at me. I laughed at myself, too. I didn't know what I was doing, and I know other people didn't know what they were doing either. We were supposed to be learning, and I think I learned my lesson with that experience. It didn't hurt anyone, but I definitely knew what *not* to do with a hand grenade.

The drill sergeants always picked on the soldiers in training. I guess they thought it was fun to haze us and make us do random things to make them laugh. One night, a drill sergeant gave me a lightning rod and asked me to go out and find steel to make a ring. I wasn't sure exactly what he wanted from me, but I couldn't say no to him. Who knows what would have happened if I'd tried! So, I did as I was told and came back with what I could find. I think he was just picking on me. I doubt he actually needed anything for any real reason. Messing with us was one of the ways our superiors made us mentally tougher — and got some good chuckles in the process.

The Army kept us pretty busy every day. We didn't have much down time to relax after the long days of training. When I would see Dewayne before bed, we would talk about what each other had done that day and how we couldn't wait to go home. Talking with him always made me feel a little closer to home. Most days, we were so exhausted, we would fall asleep while we were talking in our bunks.

At the end of basic, they told us we would have to go through more training, Advanced Individual Training (AIT). I was more annoyed than anything, but once I learned that it was training with real weapons and with a real job, I was okay with it. Most of the people I was in basic with got different MOS's, or military occupational specialties. I was supposed to go into light weapons infantry. Dewayne was going to clerk school, and Freddy was assigned to motor pool.

Regardless of your MOS, you were more than likely going to Vietnam. They needed clerks, mechanics, cooks, etc., in Vietnam, just as much as they needed infantry. Were certain MOS's a little safer than others? Sure. But no matter where you were assigned, to be in Vietnam was no picnic.

The last couple days of basic training were *a lot* different than the rest. We completed the large majority of our training, and the last few days we prepared for the graduation ceremony. Family, friends, military officers, media, and anyone interested would be attending the ceremony, and we had to look sharp.

I had a little difficulty learning the proper way to parade march. For example, when they said, "About face," I had a bad habit of turning the wrong direction, much to the disappointment of my drill sergeant. Needless to say, I was given the "opportunity" to practice ... and practice ... and then practice some more until my "about face" was as crisp as a potato chip!

The evening before graduation, they loaded us all on trucks and took us out far away from the main part of Fort Knox. They put on what I would say was better than a fireworks show. They shot everything from tanks to .50-caliber weapons and everything in between. As I mentioned, during basic training we hadn't fired weapons or seen a display of military fire power, so for us, this was an impressive display of our capabilities, and after several weeks of training, marching, running, and cleaning, anything was a welcome break. As a matter of fact, the last couple days of basic, the food got a little better. Nothing comparable to a home-cooked meal, but for the military, it wasn't that bad. Maybe we could taste the end of basic, and that just made it more bearable.

My mom and dad came to the graduation ceremony. I nailed my "about face" during parade march and was given the rank of private. It was good to see familiar faces that weren't military-related. It was good to hug my parents, to feel loved. I was now a trained private in the United States Army, about to go to war, in the best shape of my life — and I forgot all of that, if just for a few moments during that hug. I was now on leave until I was to report for AIT at Fort Polk, Louisiana. Mom, Dad, and I loaded up the car and made the two-and-a-half-hour drive home.

• • •

Once at home, I felt invincible. I was stronger mentally and physically than ever. I had two weeks before I had to go to AIT, where I would learn how to use different weapons.

I intended to make the most of being home. I was happy to see people I hadn't seen in a couple months, and I was especially happy to feel at home again. I finally was able to sleep in a comfortable bed for longer than four hours at a time. I ate better-tasting food and was able to do what I wanted. I felt better about my future, but being at home made me want to stay there forever.

When I was home, I saw Jane a couple of times. She was still in high school and her parents still weren't very fond of her dating an older man. We went out a couple of times, and it was good. She told me that even though she knew we wouldn't be able to see each other much over the next year or so, she would wait for me. That made me feel good. I was happy to be with a girl like Jane. I loved her, and I wanted to think about a future with her. That helped me a lot throughout my military experience.

Dewayne and I got this crazy idea to go to Florida between basic and AIT. We wanted to have fun together and get our minds off all the serious stuff around us. We drove Dad's old Chevy truck all the way to Daytona Beach. It was about a thirteen-hour drive each way. The two of us planned on staying for a week, just to relax.

On the third day we were there, I could tell Dewayne was getting homesick. We were lying on the beach looking up at the stars when Dewayne told me he missed his girlfriend. They were pretty serious, so I could understand why he wanted to see her, especially because we had to go to AIT soon after we got back. The next morning, Dewayne and I began the long ride home. It might have been shorter than we anticipated, but the trip was some much-needed time away. We still had time to see other people when we got home, so it all worked out in the end.

• • •

Once I reported to Fort Polk, I was there for about nine weeks with my same platoon from basic training. AIT was similar to basic except we focused mainly on how to handle and use weapons like M60s and M16s. The whole time in basic, we never were handed actual guns to use. But that was our focus now, finally.

Fort Polk was always called "Little Vietnam" because the terrain was a lot like Vietnam. I think the Army wanted us to be as prepared as we possibly could be. Looking back on it, not even similar terrain could prepare you for what you would experience over there.

Every morning before breakfast, we had to run about four miles. It was a lot, but I was in great shape, so it was easy for me. We didn't have to be as structured in AIT as we were in basic. We didn't have to clean our shoes or clothes. We were supposed to be more focused on learning how to use the weapons. During my time in AIT, I learned how to use a bazooka, a grenade, a .50-caliber, an M16, and many other weapons.

One day, our training consisted of going out in the woods with a compass and a map and finding our way back to base. I was with my squad, so there were about seven of us. We ended up getting lost and couldn't find our way back. None of us could figure out where we were, even with the resources they'd given us. At first, it was a little funny; we should have been able to put our heads together and find our way back. We weren't scared, because we knew the Army would take care of us. After all, we belonged to them and they wouldn't let us valuable young men go to waste.

It took them an entire day to find us. When they finally did, they were searching for us from a helicopter and spotted us down below. They landed the helicopter and we all hopped on and headed back to base. When we got back, we ate and rested, then went back to training soon after.

There was a graduation party at AIT before we left. I was a little bummed because Mom and Dad couldn't make it. A lot of other families came. I was just promoted to private first class, so I was even more upset about my parents not coming. While most of my buddies were celebrating with their families, I was alone. I made the most of it, though. I met some people who helped me have a good time. I was just so glad to be done and have a break from the Army for a little bit. Just knowing that was enough to get my mind off the fact that I was alone at the party.

• • •

When I came home from AIT, I felt even more like a big shot than I had after basic. I knew I'd gone through things that a lot of people couldn't have endured, and I felt like a pretty tough guy. I started carrying a switchblade like I was some kind of badass.

My friends and I liked to brag about what we'd gone through in the Army. We stayed away from the anti-war crowd and just enjoyed the fact that we'd made it through all our training.

I hung around my friends quite a bit while I was home. We thought we were invincible, hot-rodding around all the back roads. It was good to feel like regular teen-aged boys, riding around super-fast in our old cars. We thought we were cool. Toward the end of my two weeks being home, a couple of my friends and I went hot-rodding in a school zone. It was daylight and I'm sure I never thought about a cop being near. But a cop was sitting there and pulled me right over. I was arrested and put in jail for reckless operation in a school zone.

I couldn't believe I'd gotten busted. I'd been hot-rodding with friends since I got my license. This was the one time I got arrested. My parents weren't home because they were out of town, and none of my family lived near me, so I had to spend the night in jail. I knew I was in trouble, but I was hoping my trouble would get me out of going any further in the Army.

I sat in the jail holding cell thinking to myself: *Maybe this is what I wanted to happen. Maybe the Army won't keep me now that I've been arrested. Maybe this is a sign I shouldn't be in the Army.* My head kept spinning with thoughts like that.

Of course, the Army wouldn't dare waste a fit, young, already trained man, so I still had to report to Vietnam. In the back of my head, I probably knew that would be the case. I had already gone through basic and was trained for my military job. I should have known I wasn't getting out of anything.

After a court date, a fine, and a few points on my driver's license, the matter was settled. And so was my future.

I guess since the Army owned me at that point, I didn't care about much else. I didn't care what happened to me because I knew the Army also wouldn't care. They owned me, and I was just another one of their pawns. They'd spent months trying to brainwash me into wanting to kill other people, teaching me to think of them as the "bad guys." At this point, the Army could do anything they wanted with me.

Chapter Four

....

Off to War

The Army let me know by letter when I was supposed to
report for war: September 21, 1970.

I spent some time with Jane the night before I left; she and
I were both upset. Afterward, I had a few beers with friends,
then I went home and got some sleep. The next morning,
about fifty of my relatives came to see me off to the airport.
They were sad; I was scared.

I flew with my platoon from Chicago to Seattle, and no
one said much on the plane. We flew on commercial airlines,
but most of the flight was filled with other soldiers reporting
for duty. There was a Military Entrance Processing Station in
Seattle, where we stayed on the Army base for six days. We
were flying commercial again to get to Vietnam, so we had
to wait until the flight was full. In the meantime, we weren't
allowed to leave the base, so we all just sat around and wasted
time together.

We didn't have to go through any more training or preparation, so we had nothing but free time — plenty of time
to worry. Some of the guys there were starting their second
tour, and talking to them just made me even more scared.

They'd already been through this once and had seen everything I hadn't yet. They seemed like they were screwed up in the head from what they had been through. They had a much different mind-set than anyone going into this for the first time.

They told terrible stories. Stories about what they had been involved in and what they had seen. It was terrifying. I didn't want to deal with the same things they had, and I didn't want to turn out like they had, either. All I could do was hope I would have a different experience.

When we finally were able to leave for Vietnam, the commercial plane was full of about 200 soldiers. We had a layover in Anchorage, Alaska, for two hours, and I have the funniest little memory from that short stop. I bought an orange juice that cost $2. At home, that same orange juice cost eighty-nine cents. I remember telling myself how ridiculous it was to pay that much for a drink. Now, I pay that much for a Coke anywhere I go. I can't imagine how much it costs to get an orange juice in Alaska today! All these years later, that still stands out in my mind.

After we left Alaska, we had to make an unplanned stop in Japan because our plane had engine issues. We were told not to leave the barracks there, as we could be cleared to fly again at any time, night or day.

But some of the guys were getting antsy. They were tired of waiting, and they thought it was a waste of time to sit around when we were in a new place that probably had plenty of things to do. Mainly, they wanted to go to a bar. We were bored, and I imagine everyone was more than a little scared or nervous. Sitting around with no idea what would happen next or when was just adding to the tension.

The guy who initiated the whole situation was adamant about going out.

"Let's go, guys!" he hollered at us. "No one will catch us. And we deserve a beer after that long flight."

A few guys jumped on the bandwagon, but not me. None of us knew where we were or when we'd have to get back on the plane. I didn't know what would happen to a soldier if he wasn't present to report for duty, and I didn't want to find out.

The guys who went got lucky. They were gone for a couple of hours and never got caught. Truth be told, I was a little jealous. They got some food, had a few beers, and did a little partying, and it all worked out for them while I sat on the base, doing a lot of nothing.

I'd sat with a couple other guys and talked for a little while, though we didn't talk about much of anything in particular. We weren't in the best spirits because we knew what was coming. We knew we weren't getting out of anything. We were going to Vietnam to defend our country, which meant we were going to be in battle with others. It was hard to get past that. It was hard to be happy and cut up with people when we didn't know if we would make it back home.

• • •

The next morning, we were told the plane was ready. So, we got back on board and headed to our destination, Da Nang, for seven days of combat training.

This training made it all feel real. We had different equipment and resources now, and we had to do things we hadn't done in basic or AIT. Not only that, but we could hear the sounds of war — guns firing, bombs going off — while we were training. It was hitting me hard what I was about to have to do.

One of our training tasks was going through a gas chamber wearing these huge masks. I had to do it three times, because I was really struggling. The mask was too big for my face, so I had trouble keeping it on. Most people got through in one try, but not me. Once again, I was convinced I was too small for any of this to begin with.

Over the course of the week, we also did more physical training. We had to carry a heavy backpack on a trail to feel what it was like to be out on patrol with heavy guns and ammunition. Strength was the one thing I never had issues with, despite my size.

They also taught us how to tell the difference between North Vietnamese and South Vietnamese. That was tough, because you didn't want to mistake them and kill the wrong people. The South Vietnamese were our allies. We were fighting to keep Communism from spreading down from the north into the south. And I guess we hoped we could liberate the people in the north, too.

But we weren't just fighting against the North Vietnamese army. There were also the Vietcong guerrilla fighters, and they would disguise themselves as South Vietnamese in order to get closer to American soldiers. Sometimes they even involved women and children to trick us. Maybe more so than in any other war before this one, you couldn't tell who was who and what side they were on. But somehow, you had to keep yourself alive.

It was scary to learn these things; it was a lot of pressure. It's hard to know you're entering such a dangerous place with a lot of complicated elements to it. No one in their right mind wants to kill people, but somehow the Army makes you think you're supposed to.

Being over there made things feel different. It was surreal. Before we got there, it was just me and other American soldiers preparing for war. You could kind of keep it at arm's length. But once I was there and really in the thick of everything, war was closer than ever and there was no denying it. It hit me at that point that I was about to go into a life-or-death situation. I really might not make it home.

• • •

I was numb throughout the journey to our barracks at Chu Lai Air Base. There were three of us on a tiny little prop plane, going to meet our company. I wasn't sure what to feel, so I guess my mind decided to try not to feel anything. None of us talked much.

Once we arrived on base, one of the guys there taught me how to get ready and how to pack all my stuff in my backpack. Dan was from Tennessee and talked a lot about moonshine. He told me that's what he missed most about home. He'd been in Vietnam about eight or nine months, and it helped me feel better to know I had people around who were willing to help me learn. I saw Dan again about two weeks later, as he was heading home. He'd made it through his tour just as I was beginning mine.

This was the farthest I had ever been away from home, and I was scared. I didn't want to think about not seeing my friends and family again. As it turns out, Dewayne was working as a clerk in the rear area of the base, but I never saw him. And lucky him, he never saw combat.

We had one day in Chu Lai to get ready to go into the combat zone. I prepared myself the best I could, but I couldn't do a whole lot. My nerves were going crazy and my anxiety was through the roof. The unknown scared me.

• • •

On our first real day as combat soldiers, we were being dropped off in the landing zone. There were nine guys on board: One guy was operating the machine gun out the side, two were flying the helicopter, and the other six of us were being taken to fight. As soon as I stepped inside, I was nervous. I didn't know what I was getting myself into in the helicopter, much less on the ground.

The ride was about thirty minutes, and I spent the whole time looking out the window at all the rice paddies. None of us spoke, partly because we were all thinking about other things and partly because it was too loud to have a conversation.

As we arrived in the landing zone, I could hear guns firing and people yelling in the distance. It was surreal. I couldn't believe I was going into what I was hearing.

• • •

"Get your ass off the helicopter! You've gotta go!"

When someone finally did say something, it was the gunman lighting a fire under all of us. It was time.

Some of the guys didn't jump out right away, so the guys operating the helicopter pushed them. I don't think they were ready for that, but it got them moving.

Six different helicopters were dropping guys off in the landing zone, hovering just low enough for us to jump without the bird getting stuck in the tall grass. After all of us jumped out, we were ready to go into battle.

I felt fear as soon as I felt my feet hit the ground.

The members of our platoon stayed in contact with one another through the radio, deciding where we needed to go to set up a perimeter to guard.

I was the assistant gunner, which meant I carried the ammo and followed the guy with the big M60. My job was to refill his ammo when he needed it. My backpack was heavy, but after all that training, I was able to carry it with ease. The

M60 was a lot heavier. I couldn't carry it and my backpack, but I did have an M16, a much smaller, lighter gun. Each person had a weapon to protect himself.

In our backpacks, we usually carried about nine meals at a time. We didn't know when we would get back to the barracks, so we had to have enough food to be stuck out there for a while. It was usually stuff that was canned, easy to eat, and wouldn't go bad after a few days. My pack included milk, beans, spaghetti and meatballs, and some sort of dessert. Truth was, when you finally got to eat, you didn't care what it tasted like. Crappy or not, food was food.

We each also had a poncho, hand grenades, machetes, and sometimes a claymore land mine — and of course, the all-important toilet paper and cigarettes. We were allowed to put anything we wanted in our bags, but we didn't carry anything we didn't need, because of the weight. I also had a belt strapped to me with ammo for myself and for the big M60. It was all heavy, but I managed.

The first day on the battlefield, it was very hot. The Army uniform is hot enough on its own. Then add the ammo, the heavy backpack, and the summer heat, and it was almost overwhelming. All day, we used our machetes to cut down leaves and brush to get through the jungle. There wasn't much action for our platoon that day. We'd hear people on the radio who needed help, but by the time we'd get to them, the firefight would be over. We didn't see the North Vietnamese for a few more days.

We were supposed to have three days to rest and do nothing after we had gone out a few times. It was supposed to be for us to reset and recover, since we definitely didn't take care of ourselves when we were in battle. But we never did get a whole three days off. I guess the Army thought they needed us that badly.

When we did get to rest for even half a day, we were in old buildings that had cots, a kitchen, and places to sit and eat. We could drink beer, watch movies, and play cards and games. Marijuana was popular, too. There were also Vietnamese women there who would let anyone do anything to them. They were basically sex slaves for Army men, who hadn't seen a woman in months. I'm sure they were forced by someone to be there. I never took advantage of them, because it felt wrong to me. I knew a lot of guys who were into that, though.

Some of our problems getting enough rest were self-inflicted, because we'd stay up all night and drink. We'd just get carried away and lose track of time. This did not help our exhaustion. Most nights when we were out in the fields and jungle, we were lucky to get two consecutive hours of sleep. It would have been helpful to get that sleep when we at least had a cot to lie on instead of the hard ground with bugs crawling all over us.

• • •

Of all the miserable things you could experience in Vietnam, nothing compared to the monsoon we went through. We were out on a mission in the battlefield, looking for North Vietnamese soldiers. It was hot there every single day, and it was rare that we got any rain. But one day, we felt some raindrops ... and once it started, that rain didn't stop for a full two weeks. We couldn't walk in the monsoon for very long, because it was impossible to see even a few feet in front of you. We tried to stay as dry as possible since we had food in our backpacks. It was the worst rain I have ever seen in my life, and because we were out in the jungle when it started, we were stuck. We had to wait it out.

The good thing was, there wasn't much action because of the rain, so we weren't too worried about being attacked. What we *were* worried about was food. We had to ration what we had on us because we didn't know when we'd get back to the barracks. Still, we ran out. Luckily, that was just before the rain stopped, so we didn't have to go without food for very long. And thank goodness! Lots of the guys in my platoon smoked cigarettes, and they'd all run out after a few days in the field. Their nicotine fits were causing emotions to run high!

When the rain stopped, it was almost instantaneous. It just ended. Remember that scene from *Forrest Gump*? That's exactly how it happened. One day, we were in the wooded area where we had been for quite some time, and it just stopped raining. Our spirits were lifted immediately, and we went straight back to the base.

• • •

A lot of interesting stuff happened often in Vietnam. Once, we were ordered to track down a 500-pound bomb that never detonated. Apparently, the U.S. Army had dropped it out of a plane, but it hadn't gone off. Instead of leaving it and risking the North Vietnamese getting ahold of it, we had to guard it until the demolition team could get there. If the Vietnamese got to it before we did, they would use it against us or figure out how to build one just like it. When we got to the bomb and saw the crater it had left in the ground, we couldn't believe it. It was at least as big as a football field! I think we waited there for a few days until the demolition team came to detonate the bomb safely. Once they were done, so was our job there.

We had a similar situation with a helicopter not too long after that. An American helicopter went down because a propeller hit a tree. My platoon was ordered to find the helicopter and guard it. Unfortunately, everyone on board had died. We only went there to make sure the Vietnamese didn't try to steal the helicopter. That's what they did when there was something that could be of value to them.

When we found dead Vietcong, we stole anything we could from them. We would check their pockets and take their guns and other weapons they might have. The only thing I ever stole from a dead Vietcong was some jewelry. I didn't like to raid their dead bodies. Something about that felt insensitive to me.

We had to wait until the guys back at base could get a Chinook to remove the remains of the helicopter. We guarded it for about six days, and during that time, there were a couple guys who ended their tours. A helicopter came in to get them and give us some more supplies, and it also hit one of its propellers on a tree. We must not have been in a great spot for helicopters. That helicopter flipped over, but everyone survived. There were a few injuries that had to be medevacked out, but nothing too serious.

We were guarding two helicopters at this point. Even though it sounds pretty stressful, we weren't too worried about the Vietnamese coming because we were pretty close to the rear area. We got to drink beer and eat candy and food. It was like R&R in battle. When the Chinook came to get the helicopters, it got both out, and our job was done once again.

• • •

When my platoon was out on patrol, I was the rear guard, the last man in line. That could be a tricky position.

On one mission, the helicopter dropped us into a rice paddy where the grass was waist high. I ended up in a hole, which made it even harder to see as I navigated my way through. We had to climb up a hill to get out of the low ground, but by the time I got to the top, I'd lost sight of my platoon. There were three different paths leading off the hill, and I had no idea where everyone else had gone.

I started to panic a little. I picked one of the paths and took off running, yelling, "Help me!" out of sheer desperation. I still couldn't see a soul. I finally collected myself and went back to the hilltop, where I was able to make out some footprints that led me to my unit.

I was lost out there on my own for a good fifteen to thirty minutes, and the more time that passed, the madder I got. By the time I hooked back up with my platoon, I was red-hot and cussing up a storm. They told me to be quiet, that the enemy was nearby, but I kept smarting off. Again, I was ordered to shut up and get ready to shoot.

"What am I supposed to shoot at?" I asked sarcastically. "The branches out there?"

As it turned out, there were more than just branches in front of us. There were ... chickens.

They would prove to be our only engagement for the day.

• • •

On the morning of January 11, 1971, I'd been in Vietnam for four months and four days.

Our captain wanted to go back out one more time to the same place we had been before. We knew the Vietnamese soldiers had been there. We were basically putting ourselves in danger. That's the thing about war when most of your soldiers have been drafted: You have officers who are out there trying to make their careers, and you have teen-aged kids who just want to get home in one piece. Those are very different motivations — and that has consequences.

We didn't like our captain. He definitely didn't feel like "one of us." So I guess it wasn't a surprise when he made us go out on an off day. He didn't put his men first. He just wanted a body count.

Most of the time in Vietnam, our patrols would take us to places where the enemy had been but had already left. But sometimes, of course, we'd get into firefights. You could see people getting hit every day. You could always hear rifle shots and machine guns, and if you were close enough, you could even hear yelling.

Still, a lot of soldiers didn't wear the vests and protective gear because of the incredible heat. It was all just too hot and too heavy. And at a certain point, you just sort of figured you were going to get hit no matter what. Every time we went out, I'd wonder, *When is it my turn?*

• • •

I was looking around when it happened, but what's funny now is I can't remember what I was looking at exactly.

There was a loud explosion. Smoke everywhere. I couldn't see anything. But the ever-present sound of gunfire didn't let up, even through the ringing in my ears.

We'd all had a feeling we were going to get attacked, and now here we were — in the worst firefight we'd ever experienced. It was absolute havoc.

The enemy had been lying in wait for us to come through. As soon as they saw us, they detonated the mine from their hiding spot in the bush. I didn't know all of this until about two years later, when I was visited by another member of my platoon. He told me the mine was hand-detonated. We'd walked right into a trap.

Half of the 170 men in our company were injured or killed that day, including half of my eighteen-man squad. Those who survived were diagnosed with "battle fatigue" and put in the rear area until their tours ended.

For me, the Vietnam War was over. But my battles were only beginning.

....

Chapter Five

Recovery and the New Normal

I felt like a freak.

I don't remember much about the year I spent in recovery, but I do remember that. I didn't want to talk to anyone — not even my parents. I never even called them.

After my amputation surgery in Da Nang, I spent two weeks in a hospital in Guam before being sent back to the States, to Valley Forge, Pennsylvania. A bunch of us were transported on a huge military plane where our "beds" were more like hammocks. It was basically a flying hospital ward, with nurses doing their best to take care of all of us. There was one guy they were trying to keep alive until we got back to the U.S., long enough for him to see his kids — he was pretty much cut in half.

Maybe I wasn't that bad off, but I wasn't a whole man anymore. And I was in so much pain. You get your legs blown off, you're going to be in pain. I didn't want to talk to anyone. I really didn't even know *how* to talk to anyone at that point. I guess today you'd call it depression, deep depression, or post-traumatic stress disorder. I just knew I hurt, constantly, and I couldn't stop feeling like a freak.

Once I got to the hospital in Pennsylvania, it was a solid month before I would speak to anybody. I think I was still in some kind of denial about what had happened to me — and what my new life was going to look like. But there I was, in an all-amputee ward, and I had to relearn how to do everything. There was no denying it. The truth was all around me.

It was hard not to feel ashamed of myself. I couldn't even do basic things, like go to the bathroom on my own. That was absolutely the worst thing, getting on the toilet — that little bedside potty thing. I hope I die before I have to use something like that again.

Before I could even try to do things for myself, I spent four months in traction. I just sat in bed. That was it. They basically glued a sock to my skin and put weights on it, I guess to keep my bones and my blood vessels in the right places. I'm not really sure, to be honest, and it didn't matter much to me at the time. I was on plenty of pain pills, so I slept *a lot.*

The first time they took off my bandages without medication, I thought I was going to die. They gave me a piece of wood to bite on. They changed my bandages for about five months until they did the operation on my bones.

I had to have surgery for the doctors to put in what's called a bone block. They take a piece of bone from your hip and fuse it to the bottom of whatever's left of your leg so you have a base to walk on or attach a prosthesis to. For me, they could only do my right leg — the left was too short. They wanted to save as much of each leg as they could; my right leg had five and a half inches below the knee, but the left was just an inch and a half. The left one had all kinds of issues, and the doctors thought they might have to remove more of it to get it to work right. I didn't say anything, but I thought to myself, *You're not cutting more of my leg off!* And thankfully, it didn't come to that.

Before the surgery, they numbed me with a spinal needle. I couldn't sit up for three days. The first time I did, I got a terrible headache from all the blood rushing around. Worst headache I've ever had!

• • •

After a few months, I was able to get into a wheelchair. That's about the time I received my Purple Heart. There wasn't a big ceremony. Just some military higher-ups and a few photographers. They came to the hospital, pinned the Purple Heart on me, took some pictures, and that was that.

I can't recall the exact date, and my official certificate isn't any help. It dates the presentation as taking place January 10, 1971 — one day before I was actually injured in Vietnam.

• • •

Physical therapy was a special kind of torture. I had to learn to walk while my stumps were still raw and sore. I held onto the bars and walked on the bare stumps, and the pain was unbelievable! It hurt so bad, I'd start to pass out, so the therapists would give me smelling salts to revive me. The idea was amputees had to learn to walk on their own legs — whatever was still there — before getting fitted for prosthetics. You had to get stronger, and you had to learn how to use this new body you were living in. The first six months were absolutely miserable.

As awful as all this was, I always knew I was in better shape than some of the other guys in the hospital. I remember one guy in there — ninety percent of his body was burned. It made me so sad to hear him screaming on his way to get a bath. That could have been me, and I guess I was just glad it wasn't.

I know now that everything they did to you in the hospital was to prepare you to live on your own. They had to push you if you were ever going to be independent again. It was easy to get used to being taken care of.

I still remember the first time I had to get myself to the bathroom without legs. The nurse told me, "You've got to do this on your own now."

I looked at her in shock. "How am I going to do that?"

"Well, I've been taking you," she said, "so you ought to know."

I was pretty stunned! But it was clear she wasn't going to give in. I didn't get an ounce of sympathy from her that day. If I was going to get to the toilet, I was going to have to do it myself. And so I did.

The funny thing is, all these years later, the process isn't so different if I don't have my prostheses on. When I go to take a shower, I have to get out of my wheelchair, hop down on the floor, hop over into the shower, close the door, take the shower, get back out, and somehow try to get back in my wheelchair. The room has to have carpet or a rug, because I stand on my knees to get into my chair, and it hurts really bad on a hardwood floor.

Sometimes I use the toilet as a sort of stopping point between the wheelchair and the shower, but I have to be careful about that. One time, I fell back and hit my head, which sent me off the side of the toilet until I crashed my shoulder into the shower. I've only done that once, fortunately. I let my guard down, but now I'm more cautious, especially as I get older. I guess you learn some things over the course of fifty years.

. . .

I didn't have many visitors to the hospital. Mom and Dad came, and so did Jane. But I was so sick and in so much pain early on that I don't remember all the times people visited me. Mom and Dad said they came every month, but I don't recall that at all.

In those days, they wouldn't let a double amputee leave the hospital until he could walk with a cane. I spent eleven months in Valley Forge, but the first four aren't much more than a blur.

As time passed, though, I started to get to know some of the other guys on the ward. There were two long, connected hallways of about a hundred amputees. A lot of us got to know one another pretty well because we were there together for so long.

I have to admit, we got to be pretty uncontrollable. We were a bunch of young kids trying to keep ourselves occupied. Of course, we were still in the Army, so technically we still had to go by their rules. But we felt like we didn't have a whole lot left to lose.

We had one nurse who was really strict. When she had night duty, we would put shaving cream on the doorknob so it would be too slick for her to open. She'd cuss us out. She couldn't do much else!

The hospital was two stories tall with no elevators, only ramps. We'd take our wheelchairs and race on the ramps. Sometimes we'd hurt each other more than we should have. We were ornery because we knew we weren't going back to the military. What difference did it make if we got in trouble?

We played cards and stayed up all night. And we used to sneak in alcohol. We'd order food and get the delivery people to bring us a little something extra. When the nurses caught us, they'd confiscate our whiskey. But on the weekends, there wasn't much staff around, so we'd get as drunk as we could. We'd hide our liquor in the trash cans in our rooms, stuffing paper all around the bottles. I'm sure the nurses and staff knew we were drunk, but at a certain point, they either stopped worrying about it or figured there wasn't much they could do anyway. Or, maybe they knew we needed some way to blow off steam after what we'd been through — what we were still going through.

• • •

A veterans' charity sponsored some field trips for us to help us relieve stress and anxiety. Once, we went to New York City. When we got on the bus, there was a whole bunch of beer waiting for us, plus some women who helped us get around the city. We went to some shows and visited the Empire State building. A few of us even snuck out to see a burlesque show. We had to get a taxi and squeeze all three of our wheelchairs in there — that was a good trick! Then afterward, we went to our room to drink.

Another time, one of the guys and I drove to Philadelphia to be fitted for our prostheses. He had one leg missing, above the knee. The first pair of legs I got were plastic, with no padding. They were the most uncomfortable pair I've ever had, but they were the only option at that time. After we took care of our medical business, we went to the zoo and smoked weed. Drinking and smoking were how we numbed our pain. We didn't know any better, and if we had, I'm not sure we'd have cared.

Little adventures away from the hospital definitely helped improve our mood. Even though we messed around a lot in the hospital, we were well aware of the seriousness of everyone's situations. No matter how much mischief we made, there was no escaping our reality — and mine wasn't anywhere near the worst.

One guy had a hole through his leg; you could hear him hit the bone when he cleaned out the wound. Another guy was burned. Some men were triple amputees. Lots of guys would get "Dear John" letters from their wives.

We called one of our buddies "Hippy," because he'd lost a leg around the hip. One of his hands was missing, too. He had a hard time adjusting and eventually took off. Just went away one day and never came back. It was about two years before anybody found him. He was in the Salvation Army house because he didn't want to be around his family.

The ironic thing was, our captain was in the same ward I was — in a private room. I wouldn't talk to him because he'd had no business making us go on that mission that day. If it weren't for him, we probably wouldn't have been in that shape. He was a prick. I think he was still in the hospital when I got out.

· · ·

I got to go home and visit my family once during my recovery. I was excited to see them, but once I got there, I realized how uncomfortable it was to be stared at all the time. I dealt with it the best I could.

My mom wanted to do everything for me, but I wouldn't let her. I told her I had to learn to do things on my own, even though I appreciated her help. My dad understood. He tried to persuade Mom to let me take care of things and do what I needed to do.

It's hard to be in that position, to feel like you need so much help. You feel a little bit like a child, and no grown man wants that. It's hard to get past some of the negative thoughts; they never really go away. To this day, I don't feel like a complete person.

· · ·

Mom and Dad drove my car up to the hospital for me. I'd picked it out on that visit home and then left it at their house. It was a 1971 Chevy Chevelle Super Sport. It didn't have a big engine, but it looked cool. I didn't care about muscle, anyway; I just wanted a car. It gave me freedom, the ability to go where I wanted and do what I wanted. It was a year before I was very good at walking again, so that car was my lifeline.

Mom and Dad put hand controls on it for me, and the guys and I would take it from the hospital to the bars. I would blare the music all the time. My favorite song was James Taylor's version of "You've Got a Friend." That was mine and Jane's song when we were dating.

When I was finally discharged, I drove that car all the way home to Ohio from Valley Forge General Hospital — a nine-hour drive. My mom and dad had flown to Pennsylvania because they wanted to see me leave the hospital and ride home with me. I could hardly wait for them to get there. When I got the news of my discharge, I jumped up and down on my prostheses!

I was tickled to be out of the hospital and able to go home. And I was thrilled to drive that car back to Ohio, because I wanted people to know I could still do things.

I was also happy to be done with the military. When they discharge you from the hospital, that's when you're discharged from the Army.

Officially, I was "relieved from assignment and placed on the retired list" — with "retired list" typed in all caps. The

Department of the U.S. Army had deemed me 100 percent disabled, "permanently unfit for duty by reason of physical disability." "Permanently" was also in all caps.

So, as of January 19, 1972, at the ripe old age of twenty-one, I was done with the Army. On paper anyway, I was no longer their property.

Four years old in 1954, with my dad, Harold, and my brother, Lee

All dressed up for my Springboro High prom in May 1968

My official Army photo, 1970

*With my buddies Dewayne (center) and Dan
at basic training in Fort Knox, Kentucky,
May 9, 1970*

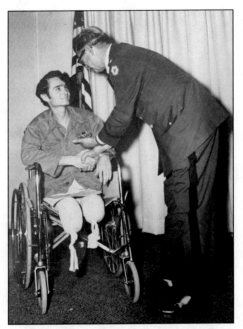

Receiving my Purple Heart while recovering from my amputations in Valley Forge, Pennsylvania, 1971

My official Purple Heart certificate

Taking Jane to her senior prom in 1972, just months before we would get married

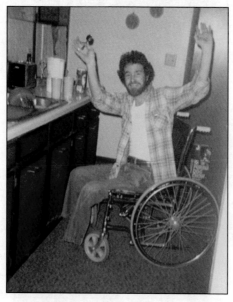

At home in 1980. To this day, I use my chair or walk on my stumps to get around the house.

I never take for granted the ability to do normal things, such as going fishing or spending time with family. In 1982, I got to visit Daytona Beach, Florida, with my dad.

I'm lucky to have a great relationship with my children today. Here I am in 1980 and 1986 with Kenny, Lori, and Amy.

At Amy's wedding in 2015, with Lori and Kenny

Celebrating Christmas in 2016 with my mom and all my grandchildren: (left to right) Kenton, Loren, Luke, Addy, Avery, Kilee, and Cameron

*Visiting family with my mom,
Francis, in 2016*

*As an Army private,
I earned a National
Defense Service Medal,
a Vietnam Service
Medal, Marksman
Badges with Rifle
Bars for the M-60 and
M-16, and of course a
Purple Heart. Today
and always, I'm proud
to be a U.S. Army
veteran.*

*Shooting pool at my seventieth
birthday party*

Chapter Six

Back to Civilian Life

When I got home to Ohio, my family had a big welcoming party for me. I was glad to be home, but seeing everyone was kind of bittersweet.

I could tell Mom was heartbroken. All of my relatives were there, and it was obvious they didn't like seeing me in that kind of shape. I was using my wheelchair at that time — I had to borrow one, because the Army hadn't given me anything but those painful prosthetic legs I was still learning to use. It was hard for people to see.

Dad didn't seem too bothered, but I think he just didn't want to talk about it or think about it.

Of course, I don't think any Vietnam veterans really had a great homecoming. The war was so controversial and unpopular, a lot of people didn't care — or flat-out didn't like it — when soldiers came back to the States.

Americans had been watching the war on the TV news every night for years. By the time I even left for Vietnam, there had already been two years of anti-war protests. Millions of people who had never been in country sure had made their minds up about what they thought and why.

Taxpayers didn't want their money wasted on an unnecessary conflict. People started calling us "killers" or even "baby killers." You never heard World War II soldiers described that way.

But that war was different. We'd been attacked on our own soil, and everyone united around the cause of defending America. It was just accepted that, in wartime, soldiers were going to have to kill or be killed. Heck, during World War II, young American boys were lying about their ages so they'd be old enough to serve! They couldn't wait to put on a uniform and fight for the USA.

Not with Vietnam. Suddenly, our own U.S. troops were the bad guys. And all we were doing is what we were told to do. The Army trained us how to kill. That's how wars are won. I'm not saying I like it, but that's just the truth of the matter. The boys in Vietnam weren't doing anything that hadn't been done by American soldiers since the country was founded.

As for me, I didn't have any desire to kill another person. In fact, I left Vietnam with no confirmed kills. It's possible I could have shot someone, but I'll never know for sure. And I'm good with that; if I knew I'd taken a life, I think I'd still feel guilty about it. That said, I was all right with the cause we were fighting for: to slow the spread of communism and free the Vietnamese people. We were trying to help ... but I guess we didn't.

Most wars nowadays don't really help anyone. Look at Afghanistan, the Taliban. We were fighting to give people a free society. That was the idea, anyway. But all these years later, war hasn't solved any of the problems. There's just been a lot of people killed or injured — that's it.

When you're at war, you do what you have to do. And that means both sides try to kill each other. That's just what war is. So, how do you know who's right?

The people who insulted U.S. soldiers ... who threw things at us ... who hated us for doing our jobs — they didn't know what they were talking about. They'll never understand what we went through.

When you got back home, the only people you could trust and rely on were your friends, because they knew you and who you'd been before you left.

• • •

Not long after I got back home, I learned that an old buddy of mine, Rob, had gone to prison for going AWOL. We'd hung out a lot when we were around fifteen, and Rob had gone into the Army like I did. When we were kids, we did all kinds of outdoorsy things together — camping, hunting, fishing. He always seemed so brave. I can remember seeing him walk over rickety little bridges, twenty feet up in the air.

I guess he wasn't so brave when it came to Vietnam.

While he was in the Army, Rob came down with appendicitis and had to be hospitalized. Apparently, he broke out of the hospital and became officially AWOL. He moved around from place to place before they finally caught up with him. They put him in front of a judge and gave him a choice: Go to Vietnam or go to prison. I don't know what he said to the judge, but about as soon as he left the courtroom, he ran off again. They caught up with him again, and this time they threw him right into military prison — in solitary confinement.

I don't agree with what Rob did, but I don't think they should have been so hard on him, either. I felt for the guy. When you see what happened to me and so many other soldiers, why would anyone want to go to war?

• • •

Dewayne got home shortly before I did, so we hung out with Deon and played cards a lot. I guess I owe it to them that I learned how to get up steps on my own. At first when we'd go out to do things, they'd help me up stairs when I needed it. But one night, we went to a friend's apartment and they just kept right on walking, leaving me on the sidewalk.

I thought for a second they'd forgotten about me, so I hollered to them. "Hey, guys, what about me? Aren't you going to help me up?"

Dewayne just shrugged, but Deon looked me square in the eye.

"It's time you learn how to do this yourself," he told me. And then he and Dewayne turned back around and walked through the front door.

I felt like I was back in Valley Forge with that nurse who wouldn't help me to the toilet. Except in this case, I was standing outside on a winter night in Ohio, freezing my ass off. Once again, I didn't think I could do it, but I didn't really have a choice. So, I found a way.

• • •

It was about a year before I could walk very well, so I used my wheelchair a lot. When I first got home, I had to wait a month to get into the VA and get my second set of prosthetic legs. When I finally did, they were much more comfortable and tailored to fit me properly. The man who made them for me was very nice, always very encouraging. Years later, after he retired, his son took over making my new legs. You have to change them every five to ten years. Now, I see *that* guy's son, so I've been through three generations making my legs.

Legs or not, I found plenty of ways to get around and have a good ol' time back at home. I was always running around partying, going to bars, taking certain drugs. My car gave me so much freedom. Walking was a challenge, but I felt very comfortable driving.

I wasn't in any hurry to find a job. I got $1,500 a month in veterans' benefits, plus $400 a month for disabled Social Security. They told me if I got a job, I'd lose the Social Security, so that deterred me from working. I knew some guys who sold their medication for extra money, too.

About the only real responsibility I had was practicing walking, essentially doing physical therapy on my own time. When I left the hospital, my legs were healed. I didn't have bandages to change or anything like that. I just had to practice using my new legs. My girlfriend, Jane, really kept me motivated. I was still so surprised that she was with me. I'd been absolutely sure she wouldn't want anything to do with me when I got home. She was good inspiration for me to get back to being close to who and what I was before I left for Vietnam.

• • •

I'd been really afraid of what Jane would think when she saw me again. I figured she wouldn't want to stick around with a guy with no legs — damaged goods and all that. But she did. I saw her right away at my welcome home party. She came right over to me and gave me a big hug.

Aside from my parents, Jane was the only person I'd seen when I was in the hospital. I'd told them not to visit, because I felt so awful about myself, but they all came together anyway. I couldn't stop them.

Jane and I had stayed in touch with letters every week or two, so she understood better than most people what I was going through, the inner demons I was fighting. It bothered me so much that I was disabled, but it didn't faze her one bit. She was just glad to have me home, alive.

Jane was only eighteen and still in high school when I got back. We started spending time together right away, mostly hanging out at her parents' house. I didn't want to burden her with having to take care of me out in public places. When we did go out for dates, we'd go to the drive-in or maybe out to dinner.

It didn't take Jane long to start talking about marriage. I loved her and I wanted to be with her, but it seemed like she was rushing things. She was ready to get out of her parents' house, while I wanted to slow down and wait a while. I was afraid of how she would react if I told her that, though. I was terrified she'd leave me, and I didn't think anybody else would want me. I didn't think I deserved for women to care about me. Jane was willing to stick by me, so I followed her lead. We got married on June 3, 1972, four months after I got home and shortly after she graduated.

• • •

Once we were married, we rented for a while before we built a wheelchair-accessible home on five acres of land, near Jane's parents. Jane loved horses, but we never got around to actually buying any. We visited her parents a lot and helped them out, because they were poor.

Jane was more or less making all the decisions, from where we would live to when we'd have kids. I listened to Jane a lot.

Not long after we got married, Jane miscarried. Supposedly she'd been on the birth-control pill, so I was shocked she'd gotten pregnant. I wasn't so certain I wanted to have children right away, but she sure did. She always said that the earlier we had our kids, the more fun we could have with them. So, I let her talk me into it. She stopped taking the pill, and she got pregnant again almost right away with our first baby, Amy.

Being a father was definitely hard for me at first. I didn't know how to handle a baby. And Amy was so little, so fragile. It felt good to hold my daughter, but I was always afraid I'd hurt her. I felt off balance, and I still wasn't great at getting around — even without a baby in my arms.

I was happy to be a father, but I had to learn what to do. I wanted to do a good job, and I couldn't tell if I was. To this day, not having my legs makes me feel like I'm no good at anything. That feeling never goes away. It's psychological, and I've had to figure out how to deal with it because I wanted to live. I never did think about suicide or anything like that. I've just dealt with it. But being a double amputee comes with all kinds of self-doubt and worries. And becoming a dad highlighted all of that for me.

A year after Amy was born, along came our son, Kenny. Not much later, we had Lori, and we knew we were done at three. Jane had her tubes tied. When Lori arrived, I felt more prepared for fatherhood — like I had a better handle on what I was doing. It felt natural and easy. Together, we settled into life as a family of five.

• • •

Jane stayed at home with the kids, and I was going to Wilmington College, studying business and history. My favorite thing to do was work on cars, but I decided to go to college instead. After all, it was free for me. I decided to become a teacher, because I thought teaching would be easy.

Boy, was I wrong! I learned that the hard way. (I would learn a lot of things the hard way over the next few years.)

I had to move around a lot in college, and walking so much gave me sores. I missed almost as much time as I went, between attending classes and student teaching. Once I got into a classroom, I couldn't handle the kids. I was teaching business and typing, and the students threw popcorn at me and made armpit noises. They even made fun of the way I talked, my accent. One time, I misspelled something on the blackboard and a girl made a point to embarrass me over it. All the other kids started laughing — it was humiliating. I kicked a few kids out of class on occasion, but I only really got their attention when I cracked my cane on one of their desks. That sure scared them! I probably should have done that more often.

Between classes, I would take my legs off to give my skin a break. The sores were painful, but I absolutely was not going to use a wheelchair in that classroom. I knew the kids would take advantage of me even more if I did that. It didn't take me long to grow tired of being made fun of, and I wasn't having it. Student teaching was all the experience I needed to know the education field wasn't for me. To heck with all that!

Otherwise, I was perfectly happy to be living a normal American life. I had a wife and kids. I'd quit drinking and partying. I only took pills for pain. We went to church as a family, and I even taught Sunday school. I didn't see my friends a lot, because I spent most of my time with Jane and the kids. I was walking well and had gotten into the groove of being a double amputee.

I was happy and content. I was doing what other people did. My life wasn't just good ... it felt complete. I felt whole.

....

Chapter Seven

Marriage, Family, Divorce, Repeat

My last year in college, Jane started going to school. She had free benefits through me, so even though it was a lot of work with three young kids, it was worth it.

Until it wasn't.

One night as I was paying the bills, I saw that our phone bill was somehow $180. It had never been that high! But we had multiple long-distance calls to a town about an hour away. I knew I hadn't made those calls, so there was only person who could have. I didn't want to be suspicious. After all, we had lots of friends. But Jane knew my friends and I knew hers ... and none of them lived in this particular town. I knew something was up, so I started doing some investigating.

My heart broke when I found it: a love letter to Jane from another man. It was in the trash, where she obviously never expected me to look. My mind began racing. *Who was this man? Where did she meet him? It had to have been at school, right? Was she cheating on me? Maybe it was a one-way street and he was the one in love with her. But what about the phone bill? If she was calling him, there was something going on. And how did she think I wouldn't see the long-distance charges? Did she want me to catch her?*

The more I thought about it, the more hurt I became — and the madder I got. This woman I trusted, who I thought had always stood by me, had been lying to me. I decided I had to confront her.

I went to Jane with the letter and threatened to take it to her parents.

"Don't you *ever* tell my mom and dad about this!" she screamed.

I reluctantly agreed. The only thing I could think to do in that moment was what I'd always done: say yes to Jane. I promised I wouldn't say anything to her parents.

But I did anyway. And my reward for telling the truth? A punch in the face from Jane's dad.

Somehow, I was the bad guy in all of this. Jane even tried to accuse me of being unfaithful with someone else. I sure wish I knew who it was! Between going to school every day and raising three kids, I didn't have time to cheat, even if I'd wanted to.

The whole mess made no sense to me. I still don't know where things went wrong. I had thought we were happy, living the American Dream. The next thing I knew, we were divorced.

Jane's betrayal hit me in the gut. I felt like I'd failed. And it brought back all the worries and fears I'd had about being a double amputee, that no one would want me and that I didn't deserve a woman's love.

My longtime love had turned her back on me. I was separated from my kids. I was so hurt. So, I turned to the things

I knew had taken away the pain before: alcohol and drugs.

• • •

It didn't take me long to get back into partying with the wrong crowd. I was out of college, my family was gone, and I was still only twenty-eight years old. I'm sure the people I hung out with thought I was just out to have a good time. But what they didn't know was that I was trying to numb my pain. Actually, maybe I didn't really know that either back then.

I definitely enjoyed my new bachelor lifestyle. Since teaching hadn't worked out, I decided to just live off my VA benefits. That gave me plenty of time to do whatever I wanted to do — and to get into plenty of trouble.

When I had my kids, I was all about being a good father. I was always there for them when they came to visit, and I never drank when I had them. We had a lot of fun together. I tried to plan special things for us to do, like visiting their grandparents or going to Chuck E. Cheese. Those three wore me out! They were always fighting, the way siblings do. And I took a lot of hits to my arms, every time we passed a Volkswagen "Punch Bug" in the car.

But when the kids weren't with me, I was a different person. I was always out with my friends, hitting the bars and getting high. Alcohol and pot were my drugs of choice. I wasn't much interested in pills.

The bonus to the drugs was the women. You don't have to worry about women when you're doing that stuff, because they like drugs, too! If you give them your drugs for free, they'll be interested in you, legs or not. Heck, they might even give you some of their stash from time to time.

About three years after my divorce, I reconnected with Marie, a girl I'd met through friends years earlier, right after I'd split with Jane. She was only sixteen when I first met her, and we'd exchanged letters for a while. She'd wanted me to take her to her prom, but of course I'd said no. I was much too old for her! Now, she was nineteen. She'd been married for a year, but her husband wasn't a good guy. After their divorce, she moved in with her brother in Wilmington.

Marie was the first person to tell me I needed to change my ways. "You've got three kids," she said, "and you need to act like it."

So, I stopped doing drugs and running around, and after about a year of dating, Marie and I got married. Four years had passed since my divorce from Jane, and I felt like I had a second chance at a normal, happy life.

Marie and I had lots of fun together. We both liked to go places, so we traveled whenever we could: Michigan, Tennessee, Niagara Falls. We went to amusement parks and visited the Grand Ole Opry and the Great Smoky Mountains. Travel became our hobby.

My kids loved Marie, and we decided to have a child of our own together. But after six months of trying, nothing. Once again, I felt like I'd failed a woman I loved. And once again, I ended up divorced.

Marie said it was because of my drinking. She said alcohol had destroyed our marriage, and I'm sure she was right. She'd wanted me to quit, but I wasn't going to let anyone else tell me what to do.

Once she was gone, I started everything up again: drugs, partying, even more drinking. I was just an alcoholic.

· · ·

I went to rehab twice after my second marriage, but that didn't help. I still had visitation with my kids, and they even came to visit me once when I did a twenty-eight-day stint. But I just never learned. After my first try at rehab, I stayed sober for all of two weeks. The second time, my sobriety lasted for eight months. I simply couldn't make myself stop drinking.

I got a bunch of DUIs — I'm not even sure how many. I'd just be driving along with a can of beer in my lap and my pot right next to me. Some of the marijuana was for me, and some I'd sell. I dealt mostly pot and coke, which were really the only drugs I used — aside from alcohol. My biggest sale was four pounds of pot in one week, for about $400.

I was never worried about being in danger from my dealers, because I always paid them on time. I carried a gun with me on occasion, but no one ever tried to hurt me. I was cautious.

I managed to stay out of trouble with the law, too. Avoiding the cops was part of the thrill. I knew that if I ever got caught, I'd go to prison and lose my Army benefits. I was always worried about that, but I had to keep dealing to keep up my own habit.

That's the thing about the drug life: Sometimes it's nice, and sometimes it's really bad. Everywhere you went, you had illegal things with you. You kept dangerous stuff in your home, even around your kids. That was just the way I lived. Most of the time, I didn't think a thing about it. But in the back of my mind, I always had a little bit of worry about getting in trouble.

You take those chances because all you care about is your next drink or your next high. You push out the bad thoughts about what could go wrong. You don't let yourself think about the other people you're putting at risk. I could have disgraced my whole family! My parents, my kids. But I just didn't care.

Was it worth selling drugs just to keep up my own habit? I ask myself that now, but back then, there was no question.

My kids had no idea — until now — about the things I was doing. But my mom and dad knew all along. They tried to get me stop, but I didn't listen.

Drugs change you. You don't know what you're doing to yourself when you're in the middle of it. You just want to drink or get high. You lie. You don't take care of your health. You can't even do basic things, like show up on time for appointments.

Most of the time, it was bad. Drugs could really make me feel terrible. And the only way to feel better was to drink another beer. Wake up with a hangover ... drink a beer ... end up drinking all day. That was my standard routine for a long, long time.

I was an alcoholic for about thirty years before I finally gave it up. One day, not long after my dad died, I woke up and just said, "I'm quitting all of this." It was one o'clock in the afternoon, a beautiful sunny day. And there I was, lying in bed, feeling awful, and wasting another day. I finally realized this was no way to live. So, I just up and quit, cold turkey.

I never looked back. I felt so much better after I quit drinking — I guess it just took me that long to mature. Something came over me, and I didn't want to do any of that stuff anymore.

• • •

I'd wasted so much time. I could have made so many better decisions. If I'd quit sooner, I'd probably still be married to Marie. I have a lot of what-ifs from a lot of years.

But at the time, it made some kind of sense. I was bored and running with the wrong crowd. And I was getting free money from the government, enough to give me some pretty nice things and let me keep living a nice, middle-class life.

When you think about it, I'm still doing that to this day, which is embarrassing. Not the drinking, but taking money from the government. I know a lot of people don't like me because I get veterans' compensation, and I can kind of understand that. I don't think I necessarily deserve it. Did I earn it? I did lose my legs for this country. And I know a lot of people who have gone to the VA and gotten compensation for things like having a heart attack. Somehow that gets tied to Vietnam, exposure to Agent Orange. I hate that. I don't like people who take the easy way out.

But some people think that's what *I* do. That bothers me still, and I guess it always will. I try to do good stuff for mankind and take care of the people around me, but I haven't been very productive with my life as far as paying taxes and stuff like that. Maybe I paid a lot of those in Vietnam. Maybe I'm still paying them.

It ain't been an easy ride, that's for sure. For decades now, I've had to endure shrapnel periodically coming out of my legs, sometimes through surgery and sometimes on its own. And every single day, things that are simple for everyone else feel like a chore to me — going to the grocery, going out to eat, visiting family. I want to be able to stand on my legs for long periods of time, but I can't. I want to be able to run and work out. It's not natural to be walking on sticks.

I want to feel normal, not nervous and anxious. People don't think of the little things that become huge for a double amputee like me.

So, have I done enough to earn my money from the government? I don't know. I just know I wish I didn't have to ask that question in the first place.

When I joined the U.S. Army, I became government property. And I guess, in some ways, that's never going to change.

Chapter Eight

Two Decades of Darkness

By the time I was thirty-six, I was twice divorced, depressed, and bored. I had no job, nothing to do, so I went back to what I'd done before I married Marie — going to bars, getting high, partying, and whatever else came along with all that on any given night.

That's how I met Annie.

She was usually at the bar I went to, and she liked to smoke pot. At that time in my life, that was good enough for me. I had nothing better to do, and Annie sucked me right in. She started coming over to my house to get high, and I started getting back into dealing to keep her satisfied.

Annie was married, but her husband was never home. He knew we were hanging out together, but he wasn't worried about me. Maybe because I was missing my legs — maybe because he just didn't care much about his marriage. He was having an affair, and Annie didn't like being around him because he didn't like to party. I was such an idiot. This whole thing was screwed up from the beginning, and I walked straight into it. Once it got started, it just kept going. And it got worse and worse and worse.

I should have known right away how messed up the situation was — how messed up Annie was. Mentally, she just wasn't right. She drank constantly but rarely ate. I swear I watched her go a month without food, just living off beer. She hardly ever slept, and she needed drugs to calm her mind and give her any kind of peace. Annie was very smart. She went to college for two years to become a nurse, but she dropped out. She could have been anything she wanted to be. But she suffered from manic depression, or what now would be known as bipolar depression, and that derailed her life.

We were friends for four or five years before she finally got divorced. I thought I was helping her somehow, but I realize now that I was just contributing to all of her problems ... and she to mine. I'm not sure I ever actually loved Annie — it was just lust. She was twelve years younger and very pretty. And she was convenient; I preferred being miserable to being alone.

I also wanted to save her. She hadn't seen her parents for almost ten years, and I convinced her to visit them and rebuild her relationship with them. That made me feel like somehow I was making her life better, fixing all the things that were broken in her. But you can't really do that for another person. I couldn't even do it for myself! Maybe taking care of her helped me take my mind off my own issues.

I kept buying Annie drugs, and I kept drinking more and more to deal with her. After close to ten years together, we got married in 1996. It was the biggest mistake I ever made.

• • •

It's hard not to think about how different my life would be if I hadn't met Annie. She seemed to have a power over men to get them to do what she wanted. And she was emotionally and physically abusive to me.

She wasted money on jewelry and clothes and shoes. I even had to refinance our house once to keep up with her bills. I made enough from my veterans' benefits and dealing drugs for us to live well, but Annie's spending was out of control and I couldn't get her to stop.

She loved my money, but she sure didn't like my kids. They were mostly grown by then, but Annie wouldn't even let me talk to them on the phone when she was around. She wouldn't let me out of her sight because she didn't like to be alone.

At the same time, she thought nothing of going off on her own for days at a time. She wouldn't tell me where she was going, what she was doing, or who she was with. When she'd come home, she'd say she didn't know or remember where she'd been or what she'd done. I'm sure she was having affairs, probably drunk and stoned out of her head. God only knows what went on.

If someone had drugs, Annie would buddy right up to them. And I accepted it. I knew that was just how she was. I told myself that I was the only one who could take care of her. Other men might want her sexually, but no one else would take care of her and protect her the way I would. She was generally a friendly person, and I thought she just didn't understand that the people she was around might hurt her. I told myself I had to be there for her. It was completely dysfunctional.

Annie and I brought out the worst in each other. I remember one day, two men approached our house and asked me to give them a ride to a nearby town. I didn't know these guys at all, but I invited them into the house for a drink. Annie and I were both already drunk and obviously not thinking clearly. Next thing I know, the two men knocked me out, raped Annie, and took off. They didn't steal anything, and Annie didn't want to press charges.

Another time, Annie went out for a "girls' night" with a coworker and never came home. I drove to the house where I'd dropped her off, but the lady who lived there told me Annie didn't want to go home. I argued a bit until a large, intimidating man came out and told me to leave. At that point, I decided I wasn't going to get beat up again on account of Annie, so I drove home. Sure enough, at eight o'clock the next morning, Annie called me and asked me to pick her up. When I got to the house, she was wearing only a robe. She didn't seem well, and when we got home and she sat down on the couch, I could see blood dripping out from under the robe. She'd been raped by the man who'd told me to leave, and she was seriously injured. I got Annie to the hospital, but I couldn't get her to press charges this time, either.

Our life seemed to consist of constantly putting ourselves in bad situations. Annie was immature and trusting and hung around with bad people. I could see trouble coming, but nothing I said could get through to Annie. When you're that deep in addiction — and dealing with a mental illness on top of it — you can't recognize what's right in front of you.

• • •

Annie rarely was sober. And that meant she was often violent. She took all of her pain and brokenness out on the people who cared for her the most.

The day of my daughter Amy's first wedding, Annie ran off again — but not before punching me and giving me a black eye. Amy had to put makeup on me so I could walk her down the aisle. Amy ended up being the one to find Annie this time...walking down the street with another guy. I got her to go home with me, and she said she felt bad about what she'd done.

We hadn't been married very long, so I wanted to make amends. I didn't want to end up divorced again. And the truth was, Annie's family didn't want to deal with her anymore. They'd already had plenty of issues with her over the years and they were done with it all. I felt like it was up to me, only me, to take care of Annie and fix her problems. And I thought she wanted to be fixed, wanted to get better.

If that was true, she sure didn't act like it. She locked me out of the house multiple times. She even stabbed me once! We were both drunk and had gotten into a fight. While I was trying to settle her down, we ended up on the floor, and Annie stabbed me in the leg with a knife. I crawled to the bathroom and tried to clean myself up, but I passed out, probably from a mix of blood loss and alcohol. When I came to, I went straight to the VA hospital, where they told me my jeans had been tight enough to stop the flow of blood and save my life. Fortunately, Annie hadn't hit any main arteries. I lied to the doctors about what had happened, told them I'd had an accident and fallen onto something. They knew better, of course. They tried to get me to tell the truth, but I wouldn't. This time, I was the one who didn't want to press charges for a crime committed against me.

When I got home, Annie didn't even offer to help me recover. In fact, we never spoke about what had happened.

The fact is, Annie did things to me all the time, and I never told anybody about it. I didn't want anyone else to know, so I dealt with it on my own. I don't know why she'd get so mad at me; I just wanted her to leave me alone. I'd try to go to sleep and she'd pour water on my head. She'd give me black eyes — probably twenty over the years. I knew my friends must have figured out what was going on.

I never got physical with Annie except in self-defense, trying to get her to cool down or wear herself out. I probably should have had her committed. I still don't understand why I stayed with her, why I never just left or got away from her. I have to take responsibility for that. I was drunk all the time, too, and I know I wasn't always the best person. Everything that happened wasn't all Annie's fault. Some of the blame is mine, too.

Annie obviously had an unhealthy need for attention — more attention than even I could give her. At one point, I did try to leave. I'd gone to my parents' house and told Annie I wasn't coming back. Her response? She shot bleach into one of her veins and threatened that if I didn't come home right away, she'd do it again. So, I went home and tried to talk to her, to calm her down and keep her from hurting herself. She finally passed out, and when she woke up, she was swollen up like a balloon. I was sure she was going to die, but she survived after spending a month in the hospital.

My parents hated Annie. They knew how deceptive she could be, and they didn't understand why I didn't leave her. They knew she was sick, but nothing they said could ever get through to me. I still don't know how to explain it. Our marriage wasn't a loving one. We'd gotten married so Annie would have insurance, though she told me later that she'd married me only because I knew people who sold drugs. It truly hurt me to hear that.

My dad died in 2001, and it was shortly afterward that I woke up on that bright, sunny afternoon and decided I was going to live my life sober. Losing my dad helped me see my own life a little more clearly.

Nothing changed for Annie, though. She kept using, and I continued to enable her. I watched her injure herself in different ways, and I was worried that she could hurt me, too. In fact, it almost cost me my life.

Annie had a lung condition — pulmonary fibrosis — and had to use oxygen. She also took morphine for back pain, and she smoked a lot. I was worried about the drugs causing her to doze off with a lit cigarette in her hand, and that's exactly what happened. She fell asleep one day, dropped her cigarette, and set our house on fire. I was in bed in the other room and was awakened by Annie yelling at me to get out. She didn't try to help me, mind you. She grabbed the cat and the dogs and ran, leaving me — without my legs on — to pull on some pants and crawl out of the burning house.

• • •

We rebuilt our home and continued to live together, in spite of everything. Annie never fully recovered from the fire; the smoke inhalation made her lung condition even worse. She died about two years later, in 2009, at the age of forty-seven, and I have to admit that I never cried for her. She calmed down a little toward the end of her life, but to me, that didn't make up for all the pain she'd caused me. We never did get divorced, though. I never felt safe with Annie, but I couldn't bring myself to walk away either.

To this day, I have nightmares about Annie and the things she did to me. Her abuse was horrifying. My life with her might have been worse than Vietnam.

I'm embarrassed about so many of the things that happened. More than twenty years with Annie, all but wasted. I wish I'd done things differently, but when two addicts get together, they can't see past their own sickness. That relationship was never anything but destructive to both of us. Maybe I couldn't see that. Or, maybe I saw it and didn't want to admit it.

What I do see now is that it's a short life. I spent so much time worrying about getting caught, wondering if I might die. I don't know how I'm living today when I think about how much I drank and how many drugs I did. I'm just glad I got through it all.

It's amazing to me that I'm still alive. I would have been dead a long time ago if I hadn't had somebody looking over me. And I believe that was God. Somebody *had* to have been there. Maybe that same figure I'd seen when I was lying on the jungle floor in Vietnam.

Chapter Nine

··

The Good Ol' Days

I did have a lot of good times over the years. I just wish I could remember more of them! I've shared some good times with good friends, and I spend quite a bit of time reminiscing about things that happened long ago — both good and bad. Mostly good, though. It's weird how easy it is to recall all the bad that happens over a lifetime, but the good times seem to slip by the wayside.

One of the things I *can* remember a lot about are the years I spent hunting. We owned some land in a rural county about an hour or so from home, and every year some friends and relatives would go deer hunting. I did that for about twenty years before giving it up after my friend John passed away. He was the one I hunted with the most, so to continue hunting without him just wouldn't have been the same. Not to mention, I was getting a little older and was starting to struggle a little more getting to and from my hunting spot. It wasn't very far from where we'd leave the truck parked, but it was getting harder to get there and back nonetheless. There was a time when I was able and fit enough to drag a deer I had shot back toward the truck. I'd have to sit on the ground, grab the deer, and drag it while scooting across the ground. Eventually, one of my friends would help me get it the rest of the way back. I never wanted to depend on them, but I knew they were always willing to help.

Sometimes we'd have a group of seven or so guys at the deer camp. We had a small cabin, and some of the guys would bring campers. We'd all hunt, then partake in a good time at night around the campfire. One morning, after one of those good times got the best of me, instead of going hunting with everyone, I stayed at camp. I told my buddies I'd keep the fire going for them and get some food ready for when they got back. Basically, I was too hung over to do anything else! Just keeping the fire going was a struggle that day. So, there I was, sitting by the fire, when all of a sudden gunfire erupted — quite a bit of it too. I looked around, wondering if it was just the pounding in my head or if I'd actually heard gunshots. Just then, a good-sized deer came trotting by, close to where I was. Luckily my shotgun was next to me, so I grabbed it, took aim, and fired. *Boom, boom, boom, boom!* I missed the deer four times! I could've thrown a rock and hit him. Maybe I should've! You don't get that close to a deer very often. I had a clear shot at it and took advantage, but there I stood, empty-handed. All I had to show for that day was the same thing I'd started with: a damn hangover.

Not too long after, three or four of my buddies came back to camp. They were cussing, laughing, and kicking themselves at the same time. They proceeded to tell me they'd all taken multiple shots at the same deer and missed. When they told me their story, they finished by saying, "At least somebody got that deer. We all heard four shots." I had to tell them, "No, that was me. I shot four times at close range; I missed the son of a bitch too." We all got a kick out of that. We've told that story a lot over the years. Good times for sure.

• • •

Whether or not anyone had a good day hunting, we all had good nights around the fire. We drank enough beer to float a battleship. We'd swap stories about hunting, women, cars, and just the good ol' days in general. One of my buddies had a Jeep, so one evening a few of them jumped in it and took it through the woods. I didn't go, and it's a good thing. They were hooting and hollering, climbing hills and whatever, and then ... *splash!* They flipped the Jeep over into the creek! Luckily, they all made it out with only a few scratches on them. If I'd been in that Jeep upside down in the water, I wouldn't have gotten out — not without help at least. I'm glad I wasn't there for that.

• • •

Overall, I did have success at hunting, and I've eaten plenty of venison over the years. My specialty was deer chili. I even made it for my kids when they were young, although I didn't tell them it was deer meat until after they were a little older.

I used to cook for my friends too. We would all help each other out with just about anything. Back in our day, it wasn't a big deal to all get together to get a project done. We stuck together through good times and bad. Sometimes — well, wait a second, most times ... okay, pretty much *every time* — there was drinking involved. There were lots of laughs and lots of poking fun at each other. But with the good comes the bad. Most of us had divorces, car wrecks, lost jobs, and DUIs. I myself had two divorces and several DUIs. I'm not saying that every bad thing I've experienced in my life is due to alcohol and drugs, but they certainly didn't help.

• • •

One time, back in 1980-something, my friends and I went to a farm that raised wild game. They sold what they called "guaranteed hunts." Basically, it was about 600 acres fenced into separate sections. We were there to hunt wild boar. The guides took me out and told me to sit in a certain spot. After a short while, sure enough, a boar came right toward me. And I got him! It was pretty thrilling because wild boar can be dangerous, and there I was, standing over the results of my first wild boar hunt. I was impressed that the guides had known exactly where to position me.

Just as I was celebrating, a pack of dogs came my way, followed by the guides. The dogs had driven the wild boar straight to me! I suppose I should have heard the dogs, but when I saw the boar, my adrenaline took over. I was so focused on a successful shot, I hadn't heard the pack of dogs tracking the animal. That's when I realized what a "guaranteed hunt" meant — and it took the thrill right out of it. All in all, I guess I got what I paid for. I got to experience the thrill of a wild boar "hunt." The adrenaline was real; the momentary fear was real. And nobody aimed and shot my gun but me. No matter how the animal had gotten within range, it was up to me to fire my gun and hit my target. I'm just glad I didn't shoot one of the dogs!

· · ·

When we weren't hunting or hanging out at one another's houses, my friends and I were running around, going to bars and sporting events and wherever else we found ourselves. Wherever we were, we were giving each other a hard time, all the time. We were all bachelors, so we were always trying to meet women — mostly in the bars. Even though I had two prosthetic legs, I was quite the dancer (self-proclaimed, of course).

One night, my friends and I found ourselves on the dance floor along with dozens of other people, mostly women. I was dancing, having a good time, showing off my moves ... and my legs flew off! They didn't connect quite as well back then as they do now. I fell flat on the ground, and my buddies had to gather up my legs from the dance floor. My friends took me back to our table, I put my legs back on, and right back to the dance floor I went. We all got a good laugh out of it. We were drinking a lot, which not only gave me plenty of courage to dance to begin with but also numbed the pain I would experience from jumping up and down.

• • •

One night I experienced a pain that had nothing to do with my prosthetics. In a crowded bar, a lady turned toward me and slapped me across the face as hard as she could! "What the hell? What did I do!?" I asked, bewildered. She just walked away and left me standing there with a hand mark across my face.

Then, I saw John. He couldn't have been laughing any harder. He was notorious for pinching a woman on her behind, just as he was slipping away — leaving the woman thinking it was the person directly behind her. In this case, that person was me. I was the butt of that joke!

John was a character. We probably deserved what he dished out to us. We gave it to him, as well. You see, John was a big guy, about 300 pounds. We had a habit of setting up someone (usually John) to think a lady might be interested in him. We'd tell him there was a woman asking about him and that she'd even bought him a drink. Then, we'd hand him a drink that we'd bought for him. We'd point out a woman, or sometimes a table of women, and send him in that direction. "Go talk to her! She bought you a drink!" Sure enough, ol' John would go over and invite himself to sit down, and we'd just sit back and watch everything unfold. It never ended well for John, but we sure got a good laugh. John was a good guy. He did end up finding everlasting love, *twice*. He was happily married for three or four years, *twice*. During one of his marriages, he came home one night and his wife had locked him out of the house. He simply left and never went back. That was John.

We were all characters of our own kind. As we got a little older, we calmed down — some sooner than others. I still see and talk to most of those friends from time to time. And the ones who have passed are still a part of my life through the good memories I have of them. We all have friends who come and go throughout our lives. Some are with us for a short time, some a long time, and some are for a lifetime. Just as my friends have come and gone in my life, I've been a part of theirs. I hope when they think of me, they have the same fond memories I have of them. I hope they refer to our time together as "back in the good ol' days."

Chapter Ten

....

Changes, for Better or Worse

I began to feel needed and useful during the years I was taking care of my mother. That's another reason to feel thankful that I got sober. My mother needed me. Just as she had always been there for me, I could finally be there for her. She lived five minutes from me, and that really helped. Caring for her gave me a sense of purpose, and it also relieved the anxiety I felt about being alone so much.

She was seventy-one when my dad died. Without him around, she was left doing everything around the house, both inside and out. That made her vulnerable to injury. She cut her leg with the weed-eater once, and I worried about all the other ways a person can hurt themselves doing day-to-day chores around their home. The fact that she lived alone made me worry about how she might hurt herself next, or the severity of the injury. Would she be able to call me when and if something happened?

So, for the next thirteen years, I took care of anything Mom needed. She couldn't drive, so I took her to doctor appointments, grocery shopping, the bank, or anywhere else she needed to go. Some days we would just go on a drive together simply to get out of the house. She enjoyed driving down to visit my kids and grandkids, and so did I. It felt good to be useful to Mom.

We had always been close, and those years made us even closer. We enjoyed each other's company, and I really did learn a lot about her and from her.

Eventually, she needed more care than I was able to give. As Mom got older, she needed more and more physical help that I couldn't provide. My legs were starting to hurt more and more, and it made it almost impossible for me to help her walk when I couldn't walk so well myself. She got to the point where she couldn't see to make coffee, and she burned herself on the stove. She wanted to come live with me, but I knew I wouldn't be able to give her the proper care. It was a difficult decision, but my brother and I agreed to place Mom in an assisted living home near my niece in West Virginia. I'm relieved to know Mom is getting the care she needs and deserves, but I miss her, and I don't like not being able to see her very often.

When Mom moved to West Virginia, that left me alone again, with no real sense of purpose. I do see Amy and Lori quite a bit, but that still leaves plenty of time to myself. My son, Kenny, lives in Mississippi. I don't see him often, but we talk on the phone quite a bit. And of course, I still talk to Deon almost daily — that hasn't changed. We hang out sometimes, too, whether we go fishing or whatever else we decide to get into. We used to go hunting, but those days are over for me. I'm just not able to do something so physical anymore.

• • •

I try to stay in touch with family and friends using social media. I also try to stay up to date with the news, and let me just say, that doesn't help my anxiety. I worry a lot about what will happen in the future. I worry a lot in general — that's part of having PTSD. Even though I haven't had a drink since 2001, I do take anxiety medication to help ease my mind. It's just another way I still feel bound to the Army, still bound to Vietnam. I may be out of Vietnam, but Vietnam is still in me.

It's hard not to feel anxious when I look at the state of the world today, the state of our country. I truly believe this is the worst I've ever seen it, and it just makes me sad.

Growing up in the Sixties, I remember well the protests and even some riots. But the division and the chaos I see today really make me nervous. Back then, there were more peaceful demonstrations. Today, not only are there protests, but apparently paid protestors. People are literally tearing up cities, ruining businesses privately owned by people who have nothing to do with their "cause." A big part of the problem, in my opinion, are media outlets that don't tell the truth. They don't report the news; they report their opinion and the version they feel you should hear and ultimately believe.

I believe many young people, middle-aged people, older people — basically all people who haven't learned enough about history nor the current state of affairs — don't fully understand what they are talking about, or what they think they're fighting for. The fact that everything is so political now seems to drive a wedge right through the heart of our society and through the heart of this great country. The times of having a constructive conversation about politics, social beliefs, etc., are gone, thrown right out the window, just like people try to do to the Constitution of the United States of America.

I worry about the direction this is all going. Hopefully there's a unified front on the horizon for our country, for all Americans to live together, peacefully, as one nation. That's what I hope for. That's what I hope everyone hopes for.

Too many people are living in the now. Too many people are about "What can I get for nothing?" or "I/we deserve this, just because." Oh, and by the way, we want it *now*.

Can we go back to being a more caring society? That's what we need. If all of these groups and organizations that are for this, not that, and vice versa could work together as Americans, maybe something positive would be the outcome.

We should be saying, "What can we do together as a country, *for* our country, that will make it better for all?" I'm not trying to steal a great quote from our thirty-fifth president, John F. Kennedy, but he did say it best when he said, "Ask not what your country can do for you, but what you can do for your country."

• • •

Unity is one of many things I learned in the Army, a "together we are stronger" kind of thing. You find a way to work as one, get along with everyone, any race, any gender, any religion, all backgrounds, whether you're from the city, suburbs, or grew up in the country. You're one unit, working toward a common goal. We have the greatest military in the greatest country in the world, and I'd like it to stay that way.

How do you change anything on one knee? Are those the proud Americans we should "look up" to? As a disabled American veteran and a double amputee, one of the ways I get around my home is on my stumps. I no longer have my lower legs or the feet I was born with. To take a shower or do other simple tasks is not so simple for me. I have to go from my wheelchair to the toilet and to the shower. On my stumps. Every day. For the last forty-nine years and counting. I don't keep my prosthetics on twenty-four/seven, because it's too painful. They aren't made for that. Whether I'm getting up for the day or ending the day by going to bed, I'm on my stumps. It's a constant reminder of my spilt blood in the jungles of Vietnam. I did that for my country. Everyone who has served in the military has done so for their country, to protect our way of life, our freedom, and our God-given rights as Americans.

Now we're kneeling?

I ask myself sometimes, *Is this what I fought for? Did I lose my legs for nothing?*

I understand it's their constitutional right to kneel, just as much as I understand it's my constitutional right to disagree. Standing for the flag as an American is a very short amount of time to put our differences aside and honor the men and women who have died for our freedom. If we can't stand together for that, it's hard to stand as one society for anything. Just my opinion. We all have different opinions, ideas, religions, beliefs, etc., and we are given those rights and privileges by the very constitution that is being dishonored.

I stand for our National Anthem. Even at home, if the National Anthem is being played for any event on television, I stand and I salute. I'm proud to do so. I may not be standing on the feet God gave me, but I *am* standing on the feet my country gave me — my stumps, the ones I earned defending this nation. People think they're "standing up" for their beliefs, but they are actually disrespecting me and every other veteran who has served in the United States Armed Forces.

• • •

I firmly believe every American should be required to serve two years in the military. That might sound surprising, considering everything I've been through as a result of Vietnam. But being in the Army teaches you some very valuable lessons. You learn what this country is all about. You learn work ethic and survival skills. You learn to be tough, to work hard, and to work together. You learn discipline. And you interact with people from all different backgrounds and cultures.

I guess the irony is that being owned by the U.S. military makes you realize how much you value being free. You belong to the government; you're their property. And once you've experienced that, you know with certainty that it's not how you want to live.

My opinions are based on my experiences. As you get older, you really do get wiser. You've lived through more, and you've learned along the way. Sometimes you learn the hard way — I certainly have. The world is complicated. People are complicated. Making mistakes is part of life, but learning from history can help cut down on some of the mistakes, or at least keep us from making the big ones over again.

• • •

To me, people who put others first are true heroes. I don't think of myself as a hero; I just did what I was told to do. But people who contribute to society — who care for others and put their own lives on the line — those are heroes. And anyone can be a hero. You don't have to have money or power. You just have to care for other people, put someone else's life ahead of yours.

....

Chapter Eleven

What Is and What Could've Been

I try to live in the moment (in my earlier years that was very obvious, now that I'm looking back), but things still haunt me about my past — things I wish I'd done and a lot of things I wish I hadn't.

With or without legs, there were a lot of potential accomplishments out there waiting for me, but I didn't apply myself. I wish I could've had that moment of clarity long before I was fifty-two. I have a lot of regrets. If I could go back in time and grab ahold of the younger version of myself and shake some sense into him, who knows what I could've achieved. I wish I'd realized long before 2001 that I was wasting my life, my time on this earth. It makes me feel downright worthless. I wish I would've stayed away from drugs and alcohol and helped the people around me who were using.

For nineteen years, I missed out on so much. I missed all of my kids' childhoods because I was a drunk. I didn't watch them play sports, either because I was drunk or because Annie wouldn't allow it. Looking back, I can see I was ashamed of myself during all of that, even while I was doing it. I felt they were ashamed of me as well. My first wife, Jane, eventually got remarried to a man named Ray. He, too, was a

Vietnam veteran, a proud Marine. I want to make sure I state that. You couldn't know Ray without knowing that. He was always there for my children. I genuinely appreciated that. I never had anything against Ray, and I was and still am glad that he fulfilled the fatherly role I couldn't. I made sure he knew that. Ray never had kids of his own, so to be a father to my children made it that much more special for him and for my kids too.

· · ·

The world sure has changed over the years. Some changes are for good, some are for worse. That being said, some things have stayed the same. For me, one thing that hasn't changed is the struggle of being a double amputee. When I first left the hospital in Pennsylvania and drove back to Ohio, like I mentioned earlier, I was proud to have made it through everything. I was beyond happy to be able to drive, have a car, and to enjoy the freedom of being mobile. The main reason for that was that I didn't feel like I had the same abilities without a car. When it came to walking, or just standing, it was very, very painful. At that time, to walk fifty or so yards was out of the question. That seemed like a marathon. Just to stand, I couldn't do it for more than fifteen minutes, and that is a stretch. Standing for fifteen minutes would take all of my energy, partly because of the concentration it took me to stand without falling, the physical effort, but mostly because of the amount of pain it caused.

The prosthetic legs I had in the Seventies definitely weren't built for comfort. But it's what I had to work with, so like many other amputees I dealt with it and made the best of what I had. Even with the prosthetics, I still used a wheelchair — and still do, especially around the house. But in public I most always walked on my prosthetic legs. Today's prosthetic limbs are much better, and there are multiple options. What I'm given through the VA are fiberglass at the top with padding, and they are fitted specifically for me. They attach at my stumps, and the bottom (the calf area and down) are carbon fiber. I have sneakers on the bottoms. The legs are much more comfortable, but standing and walking are still painful. I can still stand for no more than thirty minutes, and the farthest I can walk without taking a break is about a hundred yards or so. I still take my legs off throughout the day.

I have fallen many times around the house, and I have fallen a few times in public through the years. Not many, but it has happened. Of course, I mainly fell in public during my drinking years — that definitely didn't help matters. During that lengthy timeframe, when I fell, I had help from a couple buddies of mine: Jim Beam and Jack Daniel. Once I was walking into the bank and tripped over a rug in the lobby. I went down, and the employees who saw it happen rushed to help me up. Maybe they thought I would hold the bank liable for falling and they were hoping to prevent a lawsuit, but that never crossed my mind. I think they were just being good people willing and able to help someone in need, and they did. I was embarrassed; the only injury was to my pride. I normally use a cane when I'm out and about, but that day I didn't. My fall was no more their fault than Vietnam was. It wasn't their fault I'm a double amputee, and it wasn't their fault that I didn't take the precaution to step safely over the rug I've been walking over for thirty years.

• • •

Now that I'm seventy years old, I'm still able to do my own shopping. I do use online shopping a lot more, because it's so convenient. I don't have to walk as much in the "big box" stores that are usually mega-sized. And I must say thanks to Lori and Amy, because they do a lot of it for me. They are patient with me, and we certainly laugh a lot when they're showing me the ins and outs of online shopping. I know enough about computers to navigate around the social media I use. For me, it's the easiest way to stay in touch with friends and relatives, but as for online shopping, my daughters come in clutch for me. I am fortunate to have such wonderful kids. They're adults now, all with spouses, children, and busy lives of their own. I am grateful to say I have mended my relationships with my kids. Thankfully, they don't hold my past against me, and we are much closer now — my grandkids too. It means the world to me to have them in my life.

My kids are always trying to get me to move closer to them. As I get older, I find myself struggling with day-to-day tasks, but I don't want to be a burden to them. Although I have to admit, I do need more and more help doing things (and not just my online shopping). I have lived alone since Annie died, and there are times I don't like it. At times I get paranoid about someone breaking into my home. Being alone so much can really mess with your mind. But at the same time, I get nervous when I'm around people. Just one of the symptoms of PTSD, something I have lived with for a long time. With PTSD, you can't win. PTSD never goes away.

Living closer to my kids would make me feel less lonely and probably safer. I really think it would make them feel safer for me, as well. Like I've told them several times, I'll think about it.

• • •

Life is a struggle for most everyone at some point. It's just a fact. I suppose it's part of being human, part of life. For me and other people like me, the struggle is a little bit more consistent. I've never wished I hadn't made it home from Vietnam. There were far too many young men who didn't have the option to make that wish. I saw too many young men lose that option in front of me. To have that mind-set would have been ungrateful, even selfish. My life has been a gift. I may not have realized it at every moment, but it's a gift all the same. It was a gift to have had the childhood I had, the parents I was born to. My family has always been there for me through thick and thin, and I have close friends I owe many thanks to. My children, grandchildren — all of whom I am immensely proud of — it is all a gift.

Last but not least, it was a gift to have had the opportunity to serve my country alongside the bravest young men I ever met. They saved my life that dreadful day. I would like to think that in some way I helped them as well. In the grand scheme of what we know as a lifetime, we shared a small period of time together that shaped the rest of our lives individually — at least the ones of us lucky enough to have made it out of Vietnam alive. For the ones who didn't, God bless their souls.

For those men alone, all those years ago, I have a lot to live for. In some ways, maybe I have lived "for" those young men. Possibly, the way I've lived my life, my ups and downs, are representative of the ones who didn't get the chance. I have loved and been loved. I've had children, friends, homes. I earned an education and had the opportunity to pursue a career. I've celebrated holidays, birthdays — basically everything most people dream of when they're growing up and wish for as adults. I have had all of this in spite of myself.

Just like in the Army, failure isn't an option. You have to keep moving. Once again, I have a second chance. How many second chances do I deserve? I don't know. What I do know? I'll make this one count. And why? Because I have a lot to live for. I'm a proud Vietnam veteran, father, son, friend, and most importantly, I'm damn proud to be an American.

Conclusion

I was going to Vietnam. That was a decision I had nothing to do with. I was injured in Vietnam. That was a decision I had nothing to do with. As for the rest of my life, I had everything to do with it ... but I've persevered. I've had struggles in my life, some that most people can never fully understand. Some I don't understand myself. I've been part of a large military unit, and now I'm a unit of one. I've laughed a lot, and I've cried a lot. I've endured about every emotion a human can experience, because I'm a survivor. I may not have always done so gracefully, but I've survived. Some people who read this book might feel I have more regrets than accomplishments. But my accomplishments are the greatest part of my life. My parents, my kids, my grandkids, and the people I had the privilege of serving alongside in the United States Army are among the greatest accomplishments I could ever imagine.

What American citizen doesn't have ups and downs during their lifetime? America itself has ups and downs. But it's also the greatest country in the world. Looking back, I realize I've lived the American dream. I've made mistakes and lived to tell about them. I've suffered, and I've thrived. I can share my thoughts and views in this book because it's my right as an American. For that, I'm proud to be the property of the U.S. Army.

"The soldier is the Army. No army is better than its soldiers. The Soldier is also a citizen. In fact, the highest obligation and privilege of citizenship is that of bearing arms for one's country."
— General George S. Patton

Appendix: Resources for Veterans

U.S. Department of Veterans Affairs Veterans Crisis Line

The Veterans Crisis Line is a toll-free, confidential resource that connects veterans in crisis and their families and friends with qualified, caring U.S. Department of Veterans Affairs responders.

To receive free, confidential support, veterans and their loved ones can:

- Call **1-800-273-8255** and **Press 1**
- Chat online at **VeteransCrisisLine.net**
- Or send a text message to **838255**

These resources are available twenty-four hours a day, seven days a week, 365 days a year. Veterans do not need to be registered with the VA or enrolled in VA health care.

The responders at the Veterans Crisis Line are specially trained and experienced in helping veterans of all ages and circumstances — from those coping with mental health issues that were never addressed to recent veterans struggling with relationships or the transition back to civilian life.

Veterans Crisis Line responders provide support when these and other issues — such as chronic pain, anxiety, depression, sleeplessness, anger, and even homelessness — reach a crisis point. Some of the responders are veterans themselves and understand what veterans and their families and friends have been through.

Disabled American Veterans

DAV assists veterans in receiving the medical, disability, employment, education, and financial benefits they've earned through their service. They also provide rides to medical appointments, in addition to a variety of outreach programs. Visit dav.org.

Freedom Service Dogs of America

The organization unleashes the potential of dogs by transforming them into custom-trained, life-changing assistance dogs for people in need, including children, veterans and active-duty military, and other adults. Visit freedomservice-dogs.org.

Pat Tillman Foundation

The foundation provides resources and educational scholarship support to veterans, active service members, and their spouses. Visit pattillmanfoundation.org.

Semper Fi Fund

The group provides immediate financial assistance and lifetime support to combat-wounded, critically ill, and catastrophically injured members of all branches of the U.S. Armed Forces and their families. Visit semperfifund.org.

Stephen Siller Tunnel to Towers Foundation

The Stephen Siller Tunnel to Towers Foundation builds mortgage-free smart homes for catastrophically injured veterans. Visit tunnel2towers.org.

Vietnam Veterans Memorial Fund

As the founder of The Wall, the Vietnam Veterans Memorial Fund works to preserve the legacy of the Vietnam Veterans Memorial, to promote healing, and to educate about the impact of the Vietnam War. Visit vvmf.org.